Editorial Project Manager:
Paul Gardner

Editor in Chief:
Sharon Coan, M.S. Ed.

Art Director:
Elayne Roberts

Associate Designer:
Denise Bauer

Production Manager:
Phil Garcia

Imaging:
Ralph Olmedo, Jr.

Trademarks:
Trademarked names and graphics appear throughout this book. Instead of listing every firm and entity which owns the trademarks or inserting a trademark symbol with each mention of a trademarked name, the publisher avers that it is using the names and graphics only for editorial purposes and to the benefit of the trademarked owner with no intention of infringing upon that trademark.

Publishers:
Rachelle Cracchiolo, M.S. Ed.
Mary Dupuy Smith, M.S. Ed.

WEB BUDDY®

Software, Instructions & Projects

Author:

Debi Hooper

Teacher Created Materials, Inc.
6421 Industry Way
Westminster, CA 92683
ISBN-1-57690-190-4

©1999 Teacher Created Materials, Inc.
Made in U.S.A.

TABLE OF CONTENTS

TABLE OF CONTENTS *(cont.)*

INTRODUCTION

What is an Off-line Browser?

An Off-line Browser is a program which allows the user to download Web pages from the Internet quickly and efficiently and then store those files on diskette at the user's computer for later use. The "off-line browsing" part occurs when the user is reading those Web pages with his or her Web browsing software (such as *Netscape* or *Microsoft Internet Explorer*) while not connected to an online Internet service.

Off-line browsers have many nicknames. You may hear them called Web harvesters, retrievers, spiders, snakes, whackers, robots, or other names. Many of them have different system requirements and some have different features but they all have the same function: to download Web pages and the associated graphics, sound, and animation files from a Web site and store them on your computer in a usable form.

Why use an Off-line Browser?

There are many reasons for using an off-line browser but several of the main reasons for educators to use one include:

- Reliability of access to Web pages—you won't have to worry about losing your lesson due to a poor net connection.

- Reducing cost of online access—your classroom computer doesn't even need to have online access.

- Providing access to current resources posted online to your students via your classroom computer, which is not online.

- Managing the content your students access—keeping them on-task and assuring that they are seeing appropriate Web pages.

- Creating portable lesson resources that can be shared via a school computer network or by sharing diskettes.

What is *Web Buddy*?

According to software manufacturer DataViz, Inc., "Web Buddy is a collection of powerful, time-saving Internet utilities that works hand-in-hand with your favorite Web browser like Netscape and MS-Internet Explorer."

It lets you collect Web pages and entire sites from the Web, automatically download those pages and sites, convert them for use in your word processor, and organize the information in one central place.

Web Buddy Technical Support

For *Web Buddy* technical support contact any one of the following:
DataViz Web site: **http://www.dataviz.com**
Phone: 203-268-0030
Fax: 203-268-4345

"webster"

Why Use *Web Buddy*?

The World Wide Web is a source of an amount of educational information which has never before been seen in the history of the world. Access to that information is immediate and widespread. However, the frequent refrain from teachers has been, "It's too slow. We don't have the equipment. There is too much inappropriate information out there."

The *Web Buddy* program becomes "your browser's best friend" by retrieving those Web pages and sites and returning them to your diskettes, hard disk, or other storage device so that they can be used in your classroom later. These pages can be used on any computer capable of running a browser, whether or not that computer is online. This enables you to do extraordinary lessons in the classroom while accessing Web information at high speeds without the need for expensive wiring or fear of students' accessing inappropriate materials.

Webster doesn't stop there, however. Use *Web Buddy* to convert Web pages to your favorite word processor documents for editing and printing. This is perfect for making classroom handouts. You can even arrange your favorite Web sites with *Web Buddy*'s bookmark utility.

Ideas for Using Web Buddy

- You will find many ready-to-go lesson plans in the the "Offline Lesson Plans" section of this book. Once you have become comfortable with *Web Buddy*, try a few of these ideas.

- Schedule your favorite newspaper or weather service for weekly or daily downloads.

- Download sites about countries or states for student projects.

- For quick access to digital photos or graphics, download them ahead of time for student use.

- Download Web pages of current events for future use. Many Web sites discontinue information once it is no longer newsworthy.

- Download Web sites for presentations to school personnel about the benefits of Internet access in classrooms.

- Organize entire unit plans on Zip disk and never fear losing that information because of URL changes online.

- Keep your school's Web site on Zip disk to share at conferences and workshops.

- Save other Web pages as templates for HTML programming for student projects or lesson presentations.

- Save fun Web sites for children and use them in a lab setting to teach them about hyperlinks and Web pages.

- Convert important Web pages into word processed documents for distributing at workshops and presentations.

- Schedule downloads of sites with large quantities of graphics, movie, and sound files during the night instead of while you are trying to use the computer for other work.

- Download Web sites full of lesson plans and browse them later when you're not online.

- Download museum Web sites and take your students on virtual tours of art, science, and history museums without ever leaving the classroom.

- Take your students' favorite authors' Web sites to school with you in order for them to learn more about the authors and pick out new books to read.

- Convert online copies of historical documents into word processed documents and use them as handouts for your students.

- Once a document is converted, you can separate sections and key in study guide questions without having to key in the entire document.

- Download several Web pages with animals from different continents and have students use graphics and information to study the animals and to create their own zoo projects.

- Convert Web pages with maps or photos from different countries and print overhead transparencies on a color inkjet printer for use with your lessons.

- Schedule weekly or monthly downloads of your favorite online educational journals to read and share them while offline.

- Copy Web pages from online book and teaching resource catalogs to attach to your yearly school purchase requests or to give to your school media coordinator for possible purchase.

- Download Web sites with instructions for school projects. You're sure to have all the necessary graphics and text pages if you download the Web site rather than printing several of the pages while you are online.

- Convert Web pages with diagrams or map outlines into word processed documents and add instructions for the students to label and/or color certain parts.

USING THIS BOOK

This book has been divided into several sections in order to make learning about offline browsers such as *Web Buddy*, and using Web pages in your classroom as simple as possible.

The Getting Started section will tell you what you need to install and use *Web Buddy* and will give you step-by-step instructions for installing it on your computer. You will also be introduced to the Toolbar and *Web Buddy* Central.

The Walk Through section will include step-by-step instructions for downloading both Web pages and entire Web sites. Instructions will also be given for scheduling downloads when you are not using the computer and for converting Web pages into word processed documents.

The Web Lessons section will provide you with an assortment of unit and lesson ideas which you can use in your classrooms with your downloaded Web pages. The lessons will cover a variety of subject areas and age levels.

THE SYMBOLS

As you read through this book, you will see a series of icons to give you clues as to what the page or lesson idea is about.

 The first symbol is Webster's pawprint. He has made his mark on the main descriptive pages throughout the book.

 This is the **Page To Go** symbol from the *Web Buddy* Toolbar. It will mark lesson ideas in which the Page To Go process has been used.

 This is the **Site To Go** symbol from the *Web Buddy* Toolbar. It will mark lesson ideas in which the Site To Go process has been used.

 This is the **Schedule** symbol from the *Web Buddy* Toolbar. It will mark lesson ideas which involve scheduling on a regular basis.

 This is the **Convert** (Windows) symbol or **Translate** (Macintosh) symbol from the *Web Buddy* Toolbar. It will mark lesson ideas in which Web files have been converted into word processing pages.

 This is the **Lesson** symbol. It will mark lesson ideas which would require you or your students to create HTML documents to use in the classroom.

Appendix A will include Quick Reference Cards that you can copy and post by the computer as a quick reminder of the steps you need to follow to download Web pages and Web sites and to schedule downloads.

Appendix B will give you information about copyright status of Web sites and simple instructions for attaining permission to download material from the Internet. It will also include guidelines for citing Web site references.

GETTING STARTED

System Requirements

Web Buddy is available for both Windows 95 and Macintosh computer systems. The specifications for each are listed below.

Windows 95

4MB RAM or greater recommended
PPP, SLIP, or LAN Internet connection required

Macintosh

8–9 MB of Hard Disk Space
68020 or greater Macintosh computers or compatibles
System 7.1 or greater
2 MB RAM or greater available for *Web Buddy* alone recommended
PPP, SLIP, or LAN Internet connection required

INSTALLING WEB BUDDY ON A MACINTOSH

Insert the CD-ROM into the drive.

Double click the Installer file.

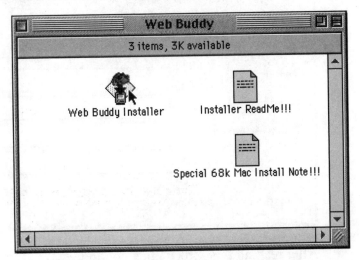

You will be prompted to agree to the Software License Agreement. Please read the agreement and then answer "Yes" if you wish to continue the installation.

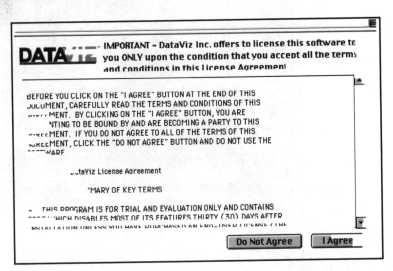

You will be asked to enter your Name, Company, Serial Number, and Activation Key. The Serial Number and Activation Key are on the registration card included in this book.

Please enter your registration info now. If you do not have a Registration Number, you may install a fully functional evaluation copy which will expire in 30 days.

To obtain a Registration Number and Activation Key, please contact DataViz :

- Phone: (800) 733-0030 or (203) 268-0030
- Fax: (203) 268-4345
- E-mail: sales@dataviz.com

Name:

Company:

Registration Number:

Activation Key:

WB-MAC 2.0

☐ **Install Evaluation Copy**   [**OK**]   [**Cancel**]

After reading this screen click continue.

WEB BUDDY™

Version 2.0

Adds Powerful Features and Utilities to Your Web Browser

Collect   web pages and entire sites from the web for convenient "offline" browsing

Schedule   Web Buddy to deliver web pages and sites right to your computer

Convert   and reuse web pages and graphics in your favorite word processor

Organize   all the information you find on the Internet in one central place

Upgrades and new feature additions are always available at:
www.dataviz.com/webbuddy

[**Continue...**]

This installation was created with Installer VISE 4.5 from MindVision Software

You will be prompted to choose a destination folder in which to install *Web Buddy*. In most instances, you should accept the default, or suggested, location.

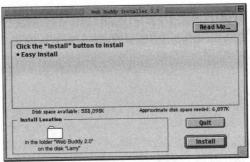

The Installation Setup program will ask that you close other programs which you may have had running before you started installing *Web Buddy*. This is a safety feature which will help the installation run smoothly and ensure that files that may need to be changed during the installation are not in use by another program at the time. Click Continue to finish the installation process.

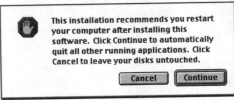

Once the installation process is complete, click on the Restart button. The software will be available for your use once your Macintosh has restarted.

The installation software will look for Iomega devices as it installs the *Web Buddy* program. If you have Iomega devices installed (such as a Zip or Jaz drive), you will see them listed here and you will need to click on the one which you will be saving files to most often. This will become your default device. If you do not use Iomega devices, choose your hard drive or other high capacity storage device as your default. It is not recomended to use a floppy drive as your default because most downloads will be too big to fit on a disk. Zip or Jaz drives are perfect solutions as they allow large amounts of memory to be stored on them.

INSTALLING WEB BUDDY ON WINDOWS 95

Insert CD-ROM into the drive.

Follow the instructions printed on the diskette label.

On a PC, using Windows 95, go to the Control Panel and double-click Add/Remove programs.

Click on Install and click on Next to install from floppy disk or CD-ROM.

The install program finds the setup.exe file on the disk and starts the *Web Buddy* install wizard.

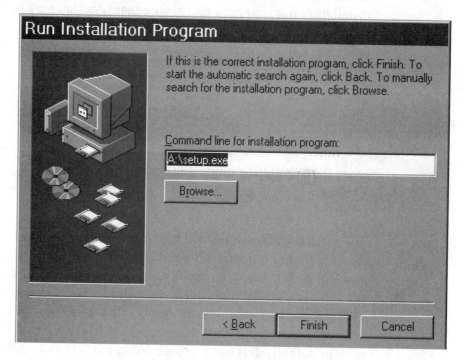

You will then see the *Web Buddy* logo graphic on your screen as the installation procedure begins.

The Installation Setup program will ask that you close other programs which you may have had running before you started installing *Web Buddy*. This is a safety feature which will help the installation run smoothly and ensure that files that may need to be changed during the installation are not in use by another program at the time.

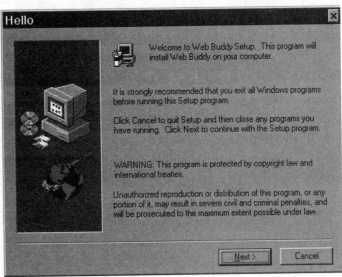

You will be asked to enter your Name, Company, Serial Number, and Activation Key. The Serial Number and Activation Key are given to you with the purchase of a licensed version of *Web Buddy*.

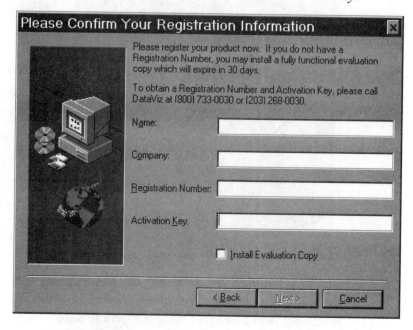

You will be prompted to agree to the Software License Agreement. Please read the agreement and then answer Yes if you wish to continue the installation.

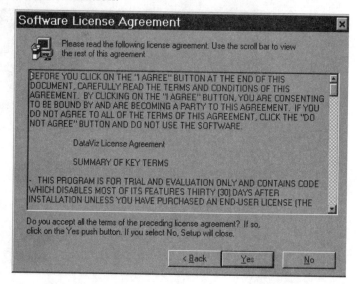

You will be prompted to choose a destination directory/folder in which to install *Web Buddy*. In most instances, you should accept the default, or suggested, location.

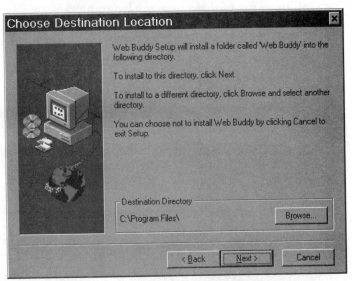

The Installation Wizard will look for Iomega devices as it installs the *Web Buddy* program.

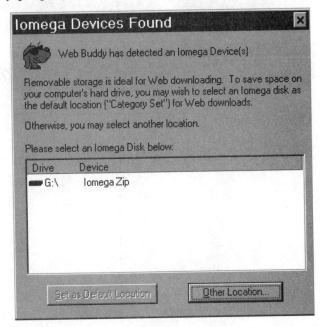

If you have Iomega devices installed, you will see them listed here and you will need to choose either your hard disk or the Iomega device (a Jaz or Zip drive) where you want to save the files most often. This will become your default device.

The Installation Wizard will also look for installed Web Browsers. You should select the one you use the most frequently to be your default browser.

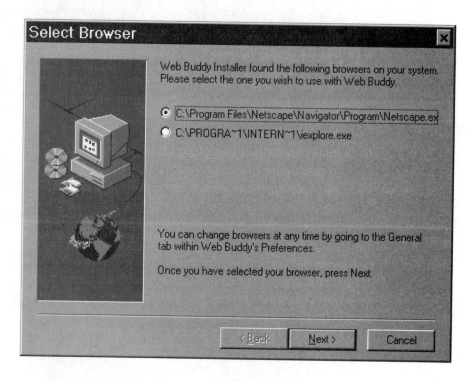

Auto *Web Buddy* Setup

From the Taskbar, you will double click on the *Web Buddy* icon in order to set up how the program will function automatically.

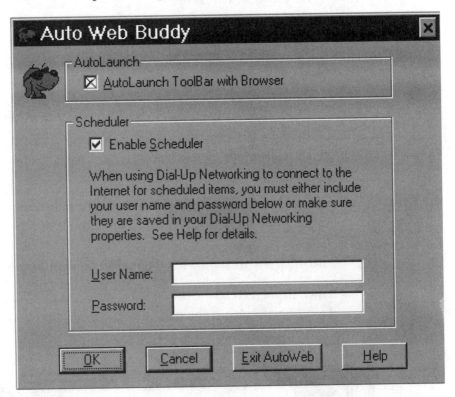

Click the box for Auto Launch if you want *Web Buddy* to start whenever you start your Web browser. Keep that box empty if you do not want it to start automatically. You will still be able to start it by double-clicking the program icon.

Enter your Internet Service dial-up User Name and Password in order to allow the *Web Buddy* Scheduler to dial your Internet connection to retrieve scheduled downloads.

WALK THROUGH—PAGE TO GO

The Whitehouse for Kids

Use Page To Go if you want to download a single Web page for use in a classroom activity or just to view offline. For this Walk Through, we will be downloading the main page of the White House for Kids Web site.

The following steps will show you how to download a single page to your computer.

1. Open your Web browser software (ex: Netscape or Microsoft Internet Explorer).

2. Locate The White House for Kids Web site by entering this URL on the location line toward the top of the browser window:

   http://www.whitehouse.gov/WH/kids/html/home.html

3. Once the screen has loaded, you should see this Web page. Don't be alarmed if the page has changed. It is doubtful that Socks will be there after elections.

If you have Auto *Web Buddy* set to Auto Launch the Tool Bar with Browser, then you should already see the toolbar on your screen.

4. If you do not have the toolbar on your screen, double-click the Tool Bar icon to start the *Web Buddy* program.

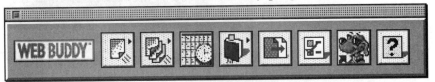

Macintosh Tool Bar (Horizontal)

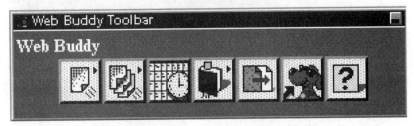

Windows Tool Bar (Horizontal)

5. Click the Page To Go button on the toolbar. That is the first button on the toolbar and looks like the icon in the margin to the left.

6. The dialog box below automatically gives the downloaded page a title. This can be edited highlighting the name and replacing it. Choose a category in which you want to save the page. You can even create new categories. Macintosh users should select New Category and type the name. Windows users should highlight the old category name and type the new name.

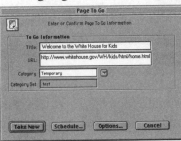

Macintosh Page To Go Screen

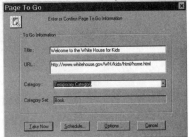

Windows Page To Go Screen

7. Since this is a small Web page, click "Take Now" and save it to the regular Temporary Category, or create a new category by highlighting the category title and typing a new category name. When the download is complete, you will hear Webster bark.

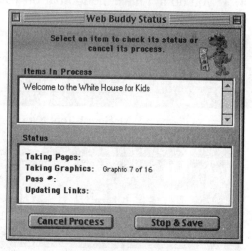

Macintosh To Go Status Screen

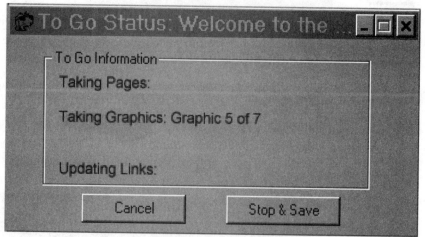

Windows To Go Status Screen

8. Now click the *Web Buddy* Central icon to start that part of the program. This is where all your Page to Go's, Site to Go's, Schedules and Bookmarks are saved and organized. Click the To Go Manager button (which looks like document pages) in the left column to see your list of downloaded Web sites.

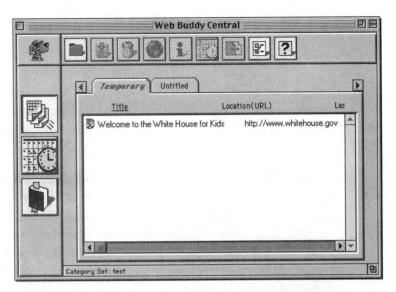

Macintosh *Web Buddy* Central Screen

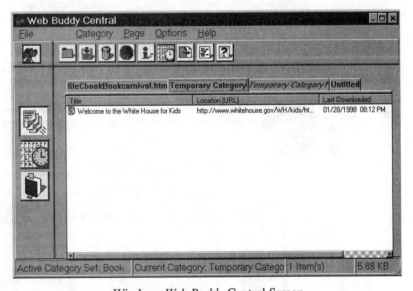

Windows *Web Buddy* Central Screen

9. If you would like to save the page to another disk, highlight the page that you wish to save, then click the disk button on the top of the window. You can then save the page to the directory/folder of your choice.

As you save the files to diskette, *Web Buddy* will change the file names accordingly.

To view a file that you saved within *Web Buddy*, go to *Web Buddy* Central and click on the To Go Manager. Select the category in which you downloaded the file, locate the file you wish to open and double click it. Your browser will open and the page will be displayed

To view the page that you have saved to a disk, simply open the Web page in your browser (*Netscape* or *Internet Explorer*). To do this, start your Web browser, choose Open File from the File menu, and navigate to the file name in the directory/folder where you had *Web Buddy* store it. Notice that the file name in the Location Bar of the browser starts with the word "file." This means that the Web page is stored on your computer.

Historic Documents

If you've ever taught lessons about a historic period in time and wanted to quickly find a speech, record of court proceedings, proclamation, historic letter, State of the Union address, or Inaugural address, then you should visit this site. It is an index to archive sources of hundreds of documents sorted by century and time period within each century.

US Historic Documents

Welcome! Here you will find nearly 500 full-text documents relating to American experience. In keeping with the web's dynamic nature, this site is ever growing. Moreover, this site contains many links to the valuable work of others. Please check all linked materials for any restrictions imposed by their owners. Students should be advised that while I will attempt to answer every query, my abilities to function as a reference desk are limited (so please be patient). Finally, the US Historic Documents site is mainlined by volunteer support staff. Consider joining the team! Many thanks to Dr. Lynn H. Nelson of the University of Kansas for pioneering this site and Branko N. Mirosavljevic for helping revise its design.

Enjoy and engage this record,

Frank E. Johnson
MidAmerica Nazarene University

US Historic Documents
http://www.mnu.edu/us_docs/

This is a perfect use of *Web Buddy*'s Page To Go utility.

1. Open your Web browser and key in the URL, **http://www.mnu.edu/us_docs/**, in the location line at the top of the browser window. This will take you to the main page above.

2. Click the buttons on that page to choose the century for the document you need.

3. Let's use Patrick Henry's "Give me Liberty, or Give me Death" speech as an example. It is listed in the 18th Century documents. Click that button from the main Web page.

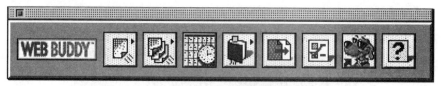

US Historic Documents *18th Century*

King William Addresses Parliament on the French Question, 31 December 1701
Robert Beverley on Bacon's Rebellion, 1704
The North Carolina Biennal Act, 1715
Benjamin Franklin: A Modest Enquiry into the Nature and Necessity of Paper Currency
Massachusetts House of Representatives on the Governor's Salary, 11 September 1728
Governor Burnet of Massachusetts on the Governor's Salary, 17 September 1728
Franklin, Benjamin: Poor Richard (1733)
Franklin, Benjamin: Poor Richard (1734)
Franklin, Benjamin: Poor Richard (1735)
Franklin, Benjamin: Poor Richard (1736)
Governor Gabriel Johnston's request to repeal the Biennal act, 18 October 1736
Franklin, Benjamin: Poor Richard (1737)
Disposition of the North Carolina Biennal Act, 1737
Franklin, Benjamin: Poor Richard (1738)
Franklin, Benjamin: Poor Richard (1739)
Franklin, Benjamin: Poor Richard (1740)
Franklin, Benjamin: Poor Richard (1741)
Franklin, Benjamin: Poor Richard (1742)
Franklin, Benjamin: Poor Richard (1743)
Franklin, Benjamin: Poor Richard (1744)

4. Click the document name and your browser will follow the link to the document you have chosen.

5. If *Web Buddy* is not already running, double-click on the *Web Buddy* Toolbar icon to start the program.

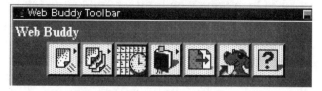

Macintosh Tool Bar

Windows Tool Bar

6. Click the Page To Go icon to start that utility.

7. You may want to make a new category with a title "Patrick Henry" or "History" depending on how you wish to organize your download (See page 21, #6). Choose Take Now from the Page To Go dialog box.

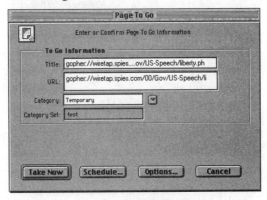

Macintosh Page To Go

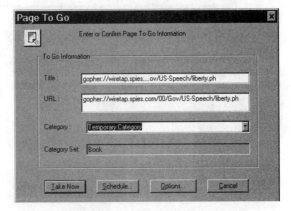

Windows Page To Go

Since it is a very small file, it will download quickly. You will hear Webster bark when the download is complete. Go to *Web Buddy* Central to view the downloaded file.

8. To view a file that you saved within *Web Buddy*, go to *Web Buddy* Central and click on the To Go Manager. Select the category in which you downloaded the file, locate the file you wish to open and double click it. Your browser will open and the page will be displayed.

9. To save to disk, go to *Web Buddy* Central by clicking the button with "Webster" on it. Look at the file list and select the file you want to save. Click the button with the disk icon on it, then choose the directory/folder where you would like to save this document.

Macintosh Save Dialog

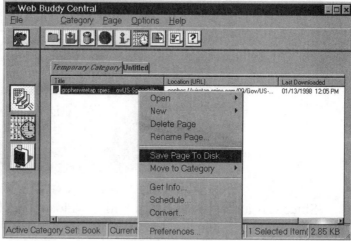

Windows Save Dialog

WALK THROUGH—SITE TO GO

Jan Brett's Home Page

Web site and artwork used in this lesson ©Jan Brett

In order to download two or more pages from a Web site, you must use *Web Buddy*'s Site To Go option. In these walk through lessons, you will follow instructions for downloading both an entire site and several pages from a site.

Jan Brett, children's book author, maintains a Web site full of teacher resources, lesson ideas, coloring pages, contests, and printable artwork. Jan is the author and illustrator of books such as *The Hat* and *The Wild Christmas Reindeer* and has retold and illustrated stories such as *Town Mouse, Country Mouse* and *The Mitten*.

If you don't have a color printer connected to the computer you are using to browse the Web, you might want to download materials from her site and take the files to a computer which does have a color printer.

Welcome to
Jan Brett's Home Page

Congratulations to the winners of the Holiday Recipe Contest. Thanks to everyone for joining the fun. I can't wait to try these recipes - I always send cookies to my daughter in Japan (mom therapy). I've listed the winners on the *Contest Winners Page*. The original artwork winning prize is at the framer. I'm looking forward to signing The Hat for the other winners.

New this month are three coloring pages from *The Mitten* on my Activities Page along with a new "How to draw an armadillo" project on the Activities Page and a postcard of the Home Page artwork on my Send a Postcard page

Jan Brett's Home Page
http://www.janbrett.com

Downloading the Entire Site

If you have the disk space and would like to browse through the entire site while offline, you could choose to download the entire site.

1. Before starting to download the Web site to your hard drive, make sure you have adequate disk space either on your hard drive or on a zip disk. You should have at least 20 Megabytes of free space for this download (plus adequate free space for your computer to function properly).

2. Double-click the *Web Buddy* Central icon to start that program.

3. Click the To Go Manager button on the top of the column on the left side of *Web Buddy* Central to see the choices at the top of the window.

4. Click Options and then Preferences to get to downloading preferences.

5. Click the To Go tab to see your preference choices.

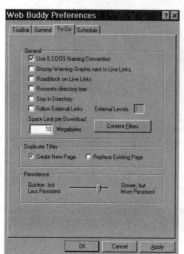
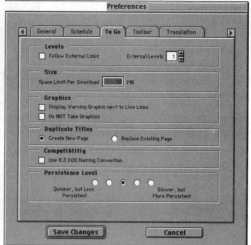

The default (or normal) space limit is 10 megabytes. In order to download this entire site, you will need to increase this since there are quite a few large graphics on the coloring pages and activities pages.

6. Change the 10 megabyte space limit to 20 megabytes. This preference will remain in effect until you change it again.

7. Click the box to have *Web Buddy* use the standard 8.3 file naming convention. (If you plan to use this site on a regular Windows operating machine, or if you might be sharing this with teachers with that operating system, Windows 95 and Macintosh are capable of using larger file names and longer extensions, but Windows 3.x requires an 8-character file name and a 3-character extension.)

8. Set the Persistence sliding bar toward the Slower but More Persistent setting so that *Web Buddy* will be more persistent in retrieving graphics.

9. Click OK to close that window.

10. Set your browser on Jan Brett's site (**http://www.janbrett.com**), and then double-click the *Web Buddy* Toolbar icon to start that program. (This may be set to automatically display.)

11. Click the Site To Go button on the Toolbar and choose a category or create a new one by entering the name into the Category box.

Web Buddy works in the background downloading the site. This means that you can work on other things on your computer while *Web Buddy* works. You can even download up to four pages or sites at the same time. The status bar will appear to tell you how the download is going. Hide or minimize it if you wish to work on other things.

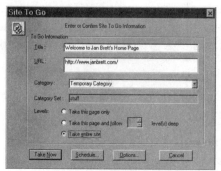 

Windows Site To Go   Macintosh Site To Go

12. If you wish to schedule the download for a later time, click on the Schedule option from the Site To Go dialog box. Be sure to choose a category in which you want to save the page. You can even create new categories. To make a new category, Macintosh users should select New Category and type the name. Windows users should highlight the old category name and type the new name.

Windows Schedule   Macintosh Schedule

13. Be sure the date is correct and enter the time that you want the download to begin. Click the circle beside "Take entire site." Then click Schedule and the site will download at your chosen time.

14. You can check the status of the download at *Web Buddy* Central's Schedule Manager. Go to the Schedule Manager by clicking on the second button in the column on the left of *Web Buddy* Central.

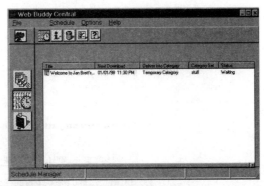

Windows Central

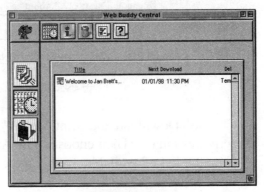

Macintosh Central

15. Once the download is complete, you will hear Webster bark.

Downloading Part of the Site

There are several classroom activities to choose from at Jan's Web site. You may decide to only download one activity or just part of the Web site.

For example, let's print a set of masks for a classroom skit about the animals in Jan's book, *The Mitten*.

The masks can be found from the Activities Pages menu on Jan's site. There is a large graphic file for a mask of each animal in the book. By having them stored on your own computer, you will save quite a bit of online time while you are printing them. This will also allow you to take the files to another computer which may have a color printer attached.

 **Activities Pages**

I've created many fun projects for you on these pages.

Download and print Masks

Download and Print Coloring Pages

Read Jan Brett's "All About" Newsnotes

Fun Projects you can make

Hear Jan Brett speak about her books

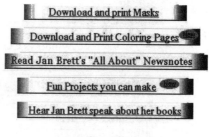

1. Choose "Download and print Masks" from the menu of activities pages. Then choose "The Animals of The Mitten" from the list of available mask pages.

The Animals of The Mitten

You can print these masks and use them for a Mitten play

The Mitten

This is a great project to use with my book *The Mitten*

These files are quite large and download slowly, but I hope that you'll be pleased by the quality

Printing Suggestions

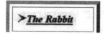
The Rabbit

2. Choose Site To Go on *Web Buddy*'s Toolbar, then choose a category.

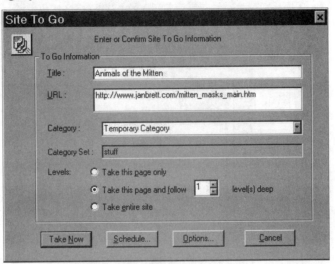

3. On the Site To Go dialog box, select Take this page and follow one level deep to download each of the masks. Be sure to choose a category in which you want to save the page. You can even create new categories. To make a new category, Macintosh users should select New Category and type the name. Windows users should highlight the old category name and type the new name. A potential category name might be "Art Projects."

Webster will bark when the download is complete.

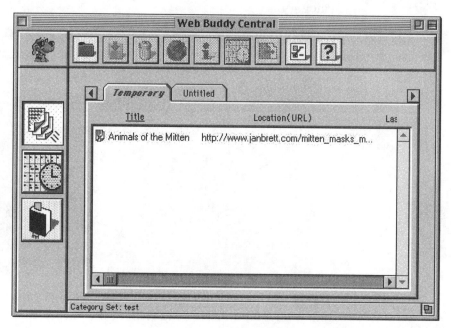

Macintosh *Web Buddy* Central

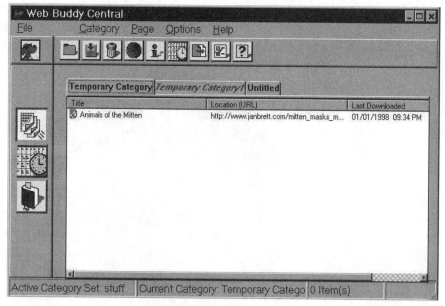

Windows *Web Buddy* Central

University of West Florida / Scenic Heights Elementary Curriculum Project

Once you find a Web site which has as many wonderful lesson plans and ideas as this one does, you'll probably want to download it and keep it as a reference guide. These are science lessons created by teachers as part of a course at the University of West Florida in the hopes of developing an educational use for the Web in elementary science.

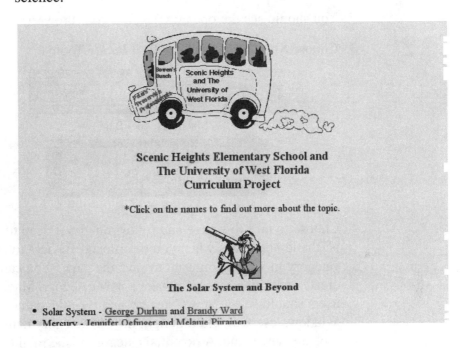

UWF-SH Curriculum Project
http://science.cc.uwf.edu/sh/curr/uwfcur.htm

This part of the Web site consists of this index page and another "level" of pages with the lessons on them.

1. Open your Web browser software. (ex: *Netscape* or *Microsoft Internet Explorer*)

2. Locate the Curriculum Project Web site by entering this URL into the location line toward the top of the browser window.

   http://science.cc.uwf.edu/sh/curr/uwfcur.htm

   You should see the opening page on your browser.

3. Choose Site To Go from the *Web Buddy* Toolbar.

Macintosh Tool Bar

WindowsTool Bar

4. Choose to take this page and follow one level deep to include all the lesson pages when you download. Be sure to choose a category in which you want to save the page. You can even create new categories. To make a new category, Macintosh users should select New Category and type the name. Windows users should highlight the old category name and type the new name. A potential category name might be "Lesson Plans."

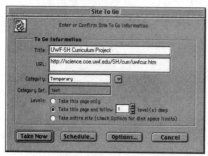

Macintosh Site To Go

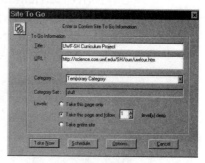

Windows Site To Go

The To Go Status dialog box will show you how many pages are being downloaded.

 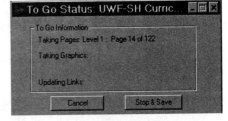

Macintosh Status   Windows Status

As you can see, there are quite a few lesson pages to download. Once you have them stored on your computer, you will be able to take your time browsing through them while you are offline or you will be able to share them with other teachers.

The To Go Status dialog box will also let you know the progress of downloading graphics files.

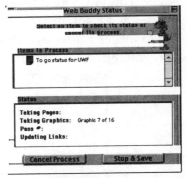

Macintosh Status

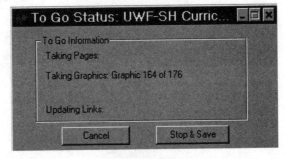

Windows Status

The *Web Buddy* program will also retry to download files if your Web connection or the destination server is slow. The Status box will keep you informed as the download continues.

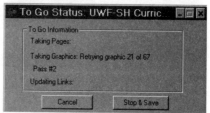

Macintosh Status   Windows Status

Web Buddy works in the background downloading the site. This means that you can work on other things on your computer while *Web Buddy* works. You can even download up to four pages or sites at the same time. The status bar will appear to tell you how the download is going. Hide or minimize it if you wish to work on other things. When finished, you will hear Webster bark.

5. Now click the *Web Buddy* Central icon to start that part of the program. This is where all your Page to Go's, Site to Go's, Schedules and Bookmarks are saved and organized. Click the To Go Manager button (which looks like document pages) in the left column to see your list of downloaded Web sites.

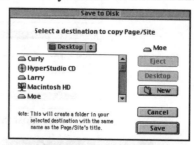

Macintosh Save To Disk

Windows Save To Disk

After you save the downloaded files to disk, you can browse through lesson plans and information such as this lesson about the Rock Cycle.

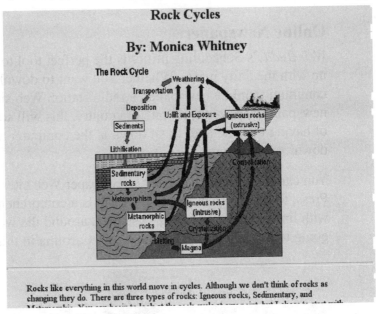

Rock Cycles

By: Monica Whitney

The Rock Cycle

Rocks like everything in this world move in cycles. Although we don't think of rocks as changing they do. There are three types of rocks: Igneous rocks, Sedimentary, and

You might also use these pages as student resource pages for research or for choosing possible science project topics.

WIND ENERGY

WHAT MAKES THE WIND?

Nobody can see the wind, but everybody can see what it does. It can make the leaves skip across the ground. The wind can make sailboats move over a lake. It can also cool your face on a hot summer day. The wind is there all day and night. When we can not feel the wind, the air is calm. The wind is always blowing even on calm days. Click HERE to read a poem about wind energy.

WHAT MAKES THE WIND BLOW?

Heat and cold make the wind blow. Here is what happens. Hot air is light, because it is light, hot air rises. You can see hot air rising when smoke comes out of a chimney. Cold air is heavier than hot air. Because cold air is heavy it sinks. Have you ever slept on a bunkbed? If you have you will have noticed that the air is always warmer in the top bunk. Now you know why. Click HERE to see more exciting things about wind energy.

WHAT KIND OF THINGS USE WIND?

Sailboats use wind energy to push their way through water. Farmers have been using wind energy for many years to pump water from wells. Today, wind is used to make electricity. Blowing wind spins the blades on a windmill. Click HERE to see photos for wind gallery.

WIND PROJECT:

There are many things you can do and make to show wind energy. You can get a pinwheel, and go

WALK THROUGH— SCHEDULED DOWNLOAD

Online Newspaper

Web Buddy's Scheduling utility is the perfect tool to help you keep up with the daily news. Whether you want to download your community online newspaper, a radio station Web site, or a newspaper from another state or country, this will solve the problem of having to remember to sit down at the computer and manually download each day.

You can use an online index of newspaper Web sites, such as Internet Press, to find the newspaper URL. It is a comprehensive Web site with links to thousands of newspapers around the world. We are going to use a newspaper from North Carolina in this example.

Monday,
January 20, 1998

Today's Weather
FORECAST: Sunny early, then becoming variably cloudy.
HIGH: 50 LOW: 34

NOW: Get the news when we get the news at The WIRE

For More News...
Check out the content

OUT FRONT

Denver stuns Green Bay

Broncos end AFC's Super Bowl drought with victory

It was set up to be a tribute to quarterback John Elway of the Denver Broncos But in the end, the final and most meaningful post-game salute

Winston-Salem JournalNow
(c) 1998 Piedmont Publishing
http://www.JournalNow.com/

You might want to locate another newspaper you would like to schedule to download and adjust these instructions for it.

1. Open your browser enter the URL below in the location line at the top of the browser window. This will take you to the main opening screen of the JournalNow newspaper.

   http://www.JournalNow.com/

2. The *Web Buddy* tool bar should be visible, but if not, double-click on the *Web Buddy* Toolbar icon in the *Web Buddy* folder to start the program.

Macintosh Tool Bar

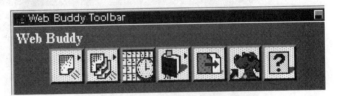

Windows Tool Bar

3. Click on the Schedule icon to start that utility.

4. Type in the time you want this to download and click in the boxes to indicate whether you want to download the front page only, a specific number of levels, or the entire site.

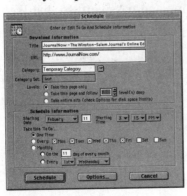

5. Choose a category or create new category where you want *Web Buddy* to put the download.

6. If you have scheduled the download for a time when you are not usually at the computer, *Web Buddy* will dial into your Internet provider for you and do the download automatically. Double-click on the Auto *Web Buddy* icon to open that dialog box. *Web Buddy* will connect, download the page, then disconnect. Be sure that the computer is left on and the AutoLaunch toolbar is checked.

7. Once you have made your choices, click the Schedule button and let *Web Buddy* do the rest.

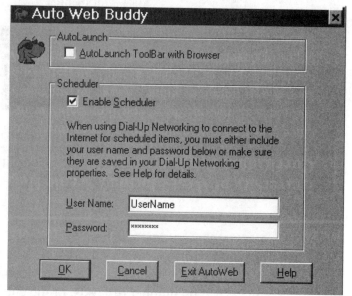

8. Insert your User name and password so that *Web Buddy* can use those when it dials in.

9. Once the download is complete, you will hear Webster bark.

10. Double-click the *Web Buddy* Central icon to start that program.

11. To view a file that you saved within *Web Buddy*, go to *Web Buddy* Central and click on the To Go Manager. Select the category in which you downloaded the file, locate the file you wish to open and double click it. Your browser will open and the page will be displayed. To save to disk, go to Web Buddy Central by clicking the button with "Webster" on it. Look at the file list and select the file you want to save by clicking it once (right clicking in the Windows version). Click the button with the disk icon on it, then choose the directory/folder where you would like to save this document.

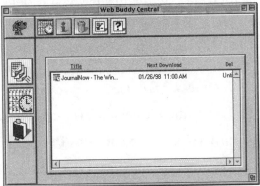

Macintosh Central

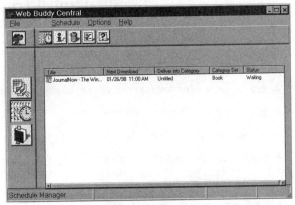

Windows Central

The Schedule Manager in *Web Buddy* Central shows a list of sites you have scheduled for download. To edit a site, you can right-click on the name (double click in the Macintosh version) and choose Info to see the dialog box again. You also right-click on the name to choose to Delete the schedule.

WALK THROUGH—CONVERTING WEB PAGES TO WORD PROCESSING DOCUMENTS

For those Web pages you would like to convert (or translate) to word processing documents, *Web Buddy*'s Convert (or Translate) utility will help you do just that.

The following steps will show you how to convert the Presidential Trivia quiz at Eduzone. You could then use this as a worksheet for your students.

1. Open your browser software (ex: *Netscape* or *Microsoft Internet Explorer*).

2. Locate the Presidential Trivia Web page at this URL:

http://www.eduzone.com/tips/PresidentTrivia/prestriv2htm.htm

3. Once the screen has loaded, you should see this Web page.

Presidential Trivia
The Eduzone wants to see how much you know about the Presidents.

1. who was the first President to be sworn into office by a woman?

2. which President ran for office unopposed?

3. who was the first President to be visit a foreign country while in office?

4. Who was the oldest President upon leaving office?

5. who were the only Presidents to be sworn into office by a former president?

6. Who won the only Presidential election to be decided by Congress?

7. which President never got married?

8. which former two Presidents died on the same day?

9. Name the Presidents who were assassinated.

10. Name the other Presidents who died in office?

11. which President created the "Bull Moose Party"?

If you have Auto *Web Buddy* set to Auto Launch the Tool Bar with the Browser, then you should already see the toolbar on your screen.

4. If you do not have the toolbar on your screen, double-click on the Tool Bar icon to start the *Web Buddy* program.

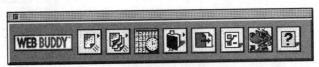

Macintosh Tool Bar (Horizontal)

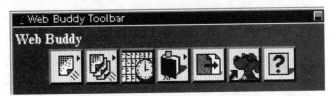

Windows Tool Bar (Horizontal)

5. Click on the Convert (Translate) button on the toolbar. That is the button that looks like the icon in the margin to the left.

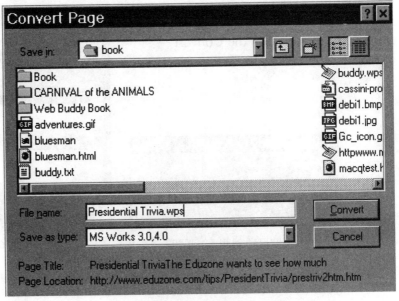

Windows Convert Page Screen

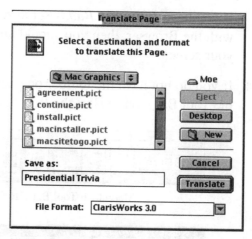

Macintosh Translate Page Screen

You will see a dialog box where you will need to make some choices about how you want the file converted and where you want it saved.

6. Choose the directory/folder where you want this new file saved.

7. Select the format of the word processing program you will be using to read the file.

8. Enter a file name for the new file.

9. Click on the Convert (Translate) button.

Windows Status Screen

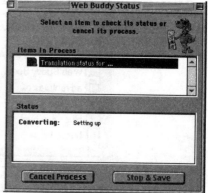

Macintosh Status Screen

You will see this status window as *Web Buddy* converts and saves your new file. When the conversion is finished, you will hear Webster bark.

You can now open your word processing program and open this file as you would any other. You can also edit and delete unwanted text and graphics and change any text formatting that you don't want.

In this document, the hypertext links convert to underlined, colored text. Simply change the formatting to undo the underlining and correct the color. You can also edit the subheading at the top of the page, but it is recommended to leave the copyright information at the bottom of the page so that you remember where you got this worksheet.

The edited worksheet now looks like this and can be duplicated for use with your students:

Presidential Trivia

1. Who was the first President to be sworn into office by a woman?

2. Which President ran for office unopposed?

3. Who was the first President to be visit a foreign country while in office?

4. Who was the oldest President upon leaving office?

5. Who were the only Presidents to be sworn into office by a former president?

6. Who won the only Presidential election to be decided by Congress?

7. Which President never got married?

8. Which former two Presidents died on the same day?

9. Name the Presidents who were assassinated.

10. Name the other Presidents who died in office?

11. Which President created the "Bull Moose Party"?

12. What does the "S" in Harry S. Truman stand for?

13. Which President was known as "Old Hickory"?

14. Name the three Presidents to die on July 4th

15. Name the two U.S. Military Academy graduates to become President

16. Which President lived the shortest time?

17. Which President was known for giving "fireside chats"?

18. Who was the first President to be nominated at a national political convention?

19. Who was the first President to leave office before his term expired without dying?

20. Which Presidents signed the Constitution?

© Copyright 1996 NYBOR® Corporation

WALK THROUGH—BOOKMARK

Education Haven

Web Buddy can help you keep track of Web site bookmarks for use when you are online. This is an easy way to organize your bookmarks to use with any Web browser.

The following steps will show you how to create a bookmark category and add Web sites to your lists.

1. Open *Web Buddy* Central and click the Bookmark button on the left-hand side of the window.

2. In *Web Buddy* Central, click on Category and then New to create a new bookmark category to add bookmarks to. There are already bookmark categories for DataViz and Iomega.

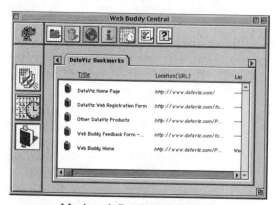

Macintosh Bookmark Central

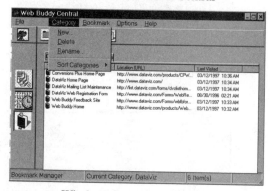

Windows Bookmark Central

3. Type a new category name in the dialog box.

Macintosh Bookmark
Category Name

Windows Bookmark
Category Name

4. Open your Web browser and locate the Web site you want to bookmark. We will use The Education Haven, an organized list of educational Web sites. Key in this URL:

The Education Haven:
http://www.geocities.com/Athens/1573/educate.html

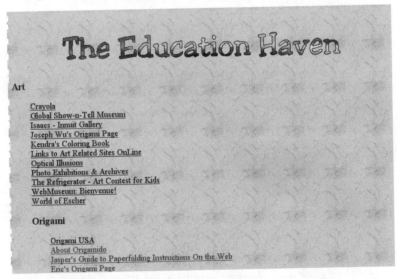

5. Open the *Web Buddy* toolbar.

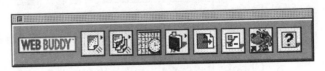

Macintosh Toolbar

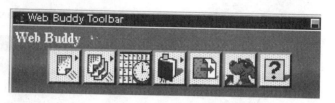

Windows Toolbar

6. Click the Bookmark button to add the Web site to the bookmark category. Select the correct category and click on Add Bookmark.

In the Windows version you can use your bookmarks within *Web Buddy* Central or you can export them to an .html file on a floppy disk and use them in another computer with any Web browser software. Both versions allow you to import bookmarks from browsers like *Netscape* and I*nternet Explorer*.

7. In *Web Buddy* Central, click Options and then Export to export the bookmark file to another disk.

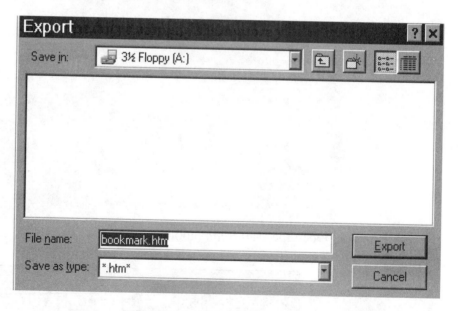

8. Choose the correct location and give your file a name that you will use to open the file within the browser software.

AESOP'S FABLES

Aesop was born a slave in about the year 620 B.C. He was owned by two different masters and was given his liberty by the second, Jadmon, as a reward for his learning and his wit. He continued to act as philosopher and teacher and created fables to teach his philosophy of life. These fables are now easily accessible online for you to use in a variety of projects.

Aesop and ME

Aesop's Fables Translated by George Fyler Townsend

Table of Contents

Why aren't these in alphabetical order ?
Simple, really. **We'd like our readers to USE the "FIND" command,** *its good practice !*

- The Wolf and the Lamb
- The Bat and the Weasels
- The Ass and the Grasshopper
- The Lion and the Mouse
- The Charcoal-Burner and the Fuller
- The Father and His Sons
- The Boy Hunting Locusts
- The Cock and the Jewel
- The Kingdom of the Lion
- The Wolf and the Crane
- The Fisherman Piping
- Hercules and the Wagoner
- The Ants and the Grasshopper
- The Traveler and His Dog

Aesop's Fables
http://i-site.on.ca/isite/education/aesop/gutenbrg/toc.html

This Web site has an archive of Aesop's fables and is collecting student submissions to include in a list of new fables. You can use the Site To Go utility to download the fables to your computer. Your access time to the groups of fables will be much shorter once they reside on your hard drive or disk. You will be able to let students search the entire list for their favorites instead of having to make print copies of just a few of them.

You could share several fables with your students and then have them write fables of their own and check the list to see if there is a similar one already written. If they can't find one that matches, then they can submit their new fable to the list and it will be posted on the Internet at this site.

The morals of Aesop's fables are still shared today in lessons from parents and teachers. Some of these tried and true morals include:

> Self-help is the best help.
> Slow but steady wins the race.
> Birds of a feather flock together.
> Fair weather friends are not worth much.
> Look before you leap.

Have students brainstorm a list of other morals they have heard and then keep that list handy as you read some of the fables and try to find the fable that corresponds to each moral they have been told.

After giving your students a chance to read just a few of Aesop's fables, let each draw a slip of paper out of a "hat" with a moral written on it. Then have him or her explain the moral with a fable of his or her own.

Primary students can listen to several of the fables and then draw pictures to illustrate them. You can copy the fables, and attach them to their illustrations, and hang them on display. You can also have them draw their illustrations on a half sheet of regular 8.5" x 11" (22 cm x 28 cm) paper and copy the pictures and fables together to create a fable book for each child to take home.

(Remember to laminate the originals and keep them in a book for the classroom.)

S.R.O.'s Aesop's Fables Page

Another organized archive of many of Aesop's fables is maintained at S.R.O.'s Aesop's Fables Page. Sung R. Oh, a student at Stevens Institute of Technology, created and maintains this Web site. Please check Teacher Created Material's Web page of URL listing updates for the new location of this site after Sung's graduation in 1999.

Exercise your mind, enrich your character.

Table of Contents:

Read one each everyday!

1-21	22-42
The Cock and the Pearl	The Frog and the Ox
The Wolf and the Lamb	Androcles
The Dog and the Shadow	The Bat, the Birds, and the Beasts
The Lion's Share	The Hart and the Hunter
The Wolf and the Crane	The Serpent and the File
The Man and the Serpent	The Man and the Wood
The Town Mouse and the Country Mouse	The Dog and the Wolf
The Fox and the Crow	The Belly and the Members
The Sick Lion	The Hart in the Ox-Stall
The Ass and the Lapdog	The Fox and the Grapes

S.R.O.'s Aesop's Fables Page
(also a .zip file of all the fables—to download and unzip to text)
http://attila.stevens-tech.edu/~soh1/aesop.html

You can use the Site To Go utility to download this index page and the following pages of story text. Converted to HTML format, these files can be used by students who want to create multimedia projects by using the fables and their scanned or computer generated illustrations.

Aesop's Fables

The Bat, the Birds, and the Beasts

A great conflict was about to come off between the Birds and the Beasts. When the two armies were collected together the Bat hesitated which to join. The Birds that passed his perch said: "Come with us"; but he said: "I am a Beast." Later on, some Beasts who were passing underneath him looked up and said: "Come with us"; but he said: "I am a Bird." Luckily at the last moment peace was made, and no battle took place, so the Bat came to the Birds and wished to join in the rejoicings, but they all turned against him and he had to fly away. He then went to the Beasts, but soon had to beat a retreat, or else they would have torn him to pieces. "Ah," said the Bat, "I see now,

"He that is neither one thing nor the other has no friends."

Go back.

Aesop's Fables—Art Project

University students at the University of Massachusetts Amherst were given traditional versions of Aesop's fables to illustrate in both a traditional style and modern style. This Web site showcases the fables and their illustrations by students in Professor Copper Giloth's class, Computing in the Fine Arts.

Aesop's Fables

Students in the course, Introduction to Computing in the Fine Arts, at <u>UMass Amherst</u> were given traditional versions of the fables, downloaded from the Internet from the PaperLess Readers Club. The students were instructed by <u>Professor Copper</u> Giloth to illustrate each fable in a traditional style and then in a modern style. Some students also wrote modern text.

🍂 credits

🍂 table of contents

Professor Copper Giloth, Department of Art
University of Massachusetts Amherst
Aesop Fables —Student Project
Art 271—Computing in the Fine Arts

 By using the Page To Go utility to download several examples of these students' work, you could present the idea to your language arts class or art class.

 Some of the students also wrote modern fables to accompany their modern illustrations. This project could be done with students of all ages. You could then scan in your students' artwork and have them create Web pages with their fables and artwork.

The Frog and the Ox  "Oh Father," said a little Frog to the big one sitting by the side of a pool, "I have seen such a terrible monster! It was big as a mountain, with horns on its head, and a long tail, and it had hoofs divided in two "	**The Frog and the Ox**  "Oh Father," said a little Frog to the big one sitting by the side of a pool, "I have seen such a terrible monster! It was big as a mountain, with horns on its head, and a long tail, and it had hoofs divided in two "

These two opening pages from Cynthia L. Cygan's project illustrate the differences in the traditional and modern stories of "The Frog and the Ox."

Other Aesop's Fables Web Sites:

Wendy's World of Stories for Children
(examples of Web pages fof fables with illustrations and sound files)
http://www.wendy.com/children/stories.html

Storyteller's Sources on the Internet
(links to other Web pages with fables and stories)
http://members.aol.com/storypage/sources.htm

Project Gutenberg E-text of Aesop's Fables
http://www.inform.umd.edu/EdRes/ReadingRoom/Fiction/Aesop/aesops-fables

Aesop's Fables
http://www.umass.edu/acco/projects/aesop/

AUTHOR OF THE MONTH

Each month could be a tribute to one of your favorite authors. You can find a wealth of information about authors on the Internet. Many have Web sites of their own online. Jan Brett's Web site is used in the walk-through section of this book.

Judy Blume's Home Base

From picture books like *The One in the Middle is the Green Kangaroo,* to books for younger readers like *"Fudge"* books, to books for older readers like *Blubber; Then Again; Maybe I Won't; Tiger Eyes;* and *Forever;* Judy Blume has written something for everyone's students.

Judy Blume's Home Base
http://www.judyblume.com/home.html

Her Web site is home to descriptions of each of her books, a biography of Judy, her tips for writing stories and books and getting published, fun "Did You Know?" answers, and news about upcoming television specials and theater presentations.

You could download this site and give your students the opportunity to read what the author has to say about her own books and to make educated choices about their next reading selections.

Have your students write their own book descriptions and post them on a bulletin board near your computer. You could then use them in a compare/contrast activity with the class.

Learning About Gary Paulsen

Gary Paulsen is another author you could put in the Author-of-the-Month spotlight. There are several sites online about his books.

LEARNING ABOUT GARY PAULSEN

Compiled by Jan Johnson, Terrie Katz, Lynn Makler, and Gina Mitgang with Kay Vandergrift in Young Adult Literature

We have compiled information about Gary Paulsen, and his work, so you can learn more about this famous young adult author.

For additional information on Gary Paulsen

Kay Vandergrift's Web Site about Gary Paulsen
http://www.scils.rutgers.edu/special/kay/paulsen.html

This site contains a biography of Gary Paulsen, author of books such as *Hatchet, The River,* and *Dancing Carl.* There is information about his written works including juvenile fiction and nonfiction, plays, and literary awards he has won. The team of people who worked on this Web site have also included reviews of several of his books.

You may want to have your students read and review his books before they read others' reviews or have them read the reviews in hopes of selecting one of his books to read.

Student book reviews would also make a terrific Web site topic. That could be a yearly project. By creating a simple index page and a page for each author as your students read books by him or her, you could start a growing project to share with other classes within your school and on the Internet.

Carol Hurst's Children's Literature Site

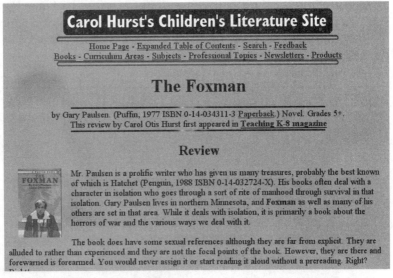

Carol Hurst's Children's Literature Site
http://www.carolhurst.com/~rebotis/titles/foxman.html

Carol's Web site offers book reviews about children's literature. There is an extensive list of authors and illustrators whose books are included. The books have also been organized by subject and by themes such as:

> Appalachia
> Color
> Families
> Farms
> Food
> Native Americans
> Quilts
> Rivers
> Time
> Trains

Gary Paulsen's *Foxman* is categorized in the U. S. History subject area. If the "Author of the Month" idea doesn't appeal to you, you might want to consider using a theme or subject approach such as the groupings at this Web site.

Carol's site offers book reviews of literature from many different authors, including this one about *Foxman* by Gary Paulsen. Along with the review, there are lists of Things to Notice and Talk About and Activities.

- The Foxman says at one point, "Science kills beauty." What does he mean? What is his example of knowledge ruining wonder? What are some other examples?

- Talk about the effects on both boys of knowing the Foxman. Why is Carl's reaction different than his cousin's? What will change in the boy's life after this book? Will he stay in the north? with the family? alone? Will he go back to his alcoholic parents?

- Finally, there is the burning of the cabin with the Foxman and all he owns inside. Is that what Foxman wanted? Why did the boy take only the fox pelt? Was he right?

Activities

- Another quote says that the storytellers are "plucking roses from manure." What about that one? Can you cite examples of it in the book and in life?

- There is violence throughout this anti-war novel. Pick out the references to it and debate their cause and effects.

- Speaking of alcoholism, investigate Alanon and Alateen. Could they have helped the boy?

- The battle of Verdun in World War I is talked about in the book. Find out what you can about it. We're hearing a lot about poison gas now in the Middle East. What was said about it then? Why was it outlawed? Can there be rules to war? Who makes the rules?

You can use the Page To Go utility to download this page with the book review and lesson ideas, then take it to your class to use. You might want to convert it into a document to use in your word processor. That would be a good idea if you are including it with materials you might be printing and keeping in a lesson file.

The House of Usher: Edgar Allan Poe (1809-1849)

If you decide to use Peter Forrest's Web site, The House of Usher, to showcase Edgar Allen Poe as the author of the month. You might want to choose October as the month. The opening Web page greets you with the eerie *Addams Family Waltz* by Marc Shaiman from the 1991 movie. This sets the stage for a journey into learning about the macabre author and poet.

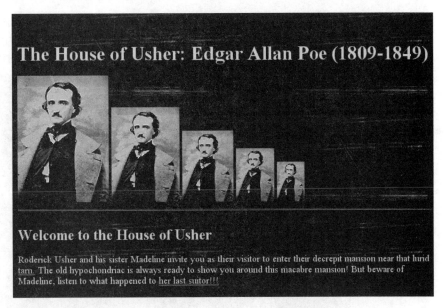

The House of Usher: Edgar Allan Poe (1809–1849)
http://www.comnet.ca/~forrest/

The information about Poe is presented in a way that will capture your students' attention as soon as they visit the Web site. For example, his homes and present resting place are described as his favorite haunts.

Several of the poems have been reformatted into Web pages with backgrounds graphics and music. The poems also have hypertext links to other information that clarifies the poem for the reader.

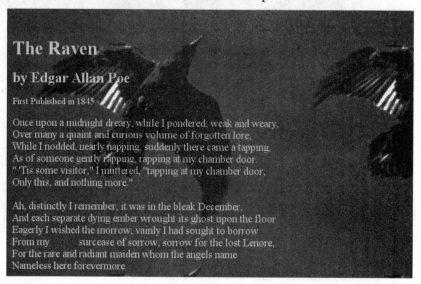

The Raven

by Edgar Allan Poe

First Published in 1845

Once upon a midnight dreary, while I pondered, weak and weary,
Over many a quaint and curious volume of forgotten lore,
While I nodded, nearly napping, suddenly there came a tapping,
As of someone gently rapping, rapping at my chamber door.
" 'Tis some visitor," I muttered, "tapping at my chamber door;
Only this, and nothing more."

Ah, distinctly I remember, it was in the bleak December,
And each separate dying ember wrought its ghost upon the floor.
Eagerly I wished the morrow; vainly I had sought to borrow
From my   surcease of sorrow, sorrow for the lost Lenore,.
For the rare and radiant maiden whom the angels name
Nameless here forevermore.

This would be a good project for teams of students to create. The Web site has links to almost all of Poe's work through Virginia Polytechnic Institute and State University's gopher service. These will download if you use the Site To Go utility and set the options to follow external links. They will be in simple text format but will be easily accessible for your students to copy and paste into their projects.

They can look at the coding for these pages and see how the background graphics and sound have been added. They can also find graphics and sounds to illustrate their poem pages. They could also add links to parts of the poems or stories that needed extra explanation.

Although most of the information at this Web site is actually part of this site, there are some external links that you may want to explore, as well. You should especially take your students on a virtual tour of the Poe Museum in Richmond, Virginia at this Web site:

http://www.poemuseum.org/

Helen Ketteman—Helen's Bookshelf

The Books

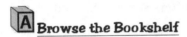
A Browse the Bookshelf

B Upcoming Books

C Order Helen's Books

Helen Ketteman Home Page
http://www.book-promotions.com/ketteman/

Helen's Web site includes information about the author, her books, as well as lesson plans for integrating her books into different curriculum areas. There are also printable handouts for several of her books. You can use *Web Buddy*'s Page To Go option or the Convert option to download these pages in order to print them for your students.

Other Author Web Sites:

Young Adult Authors & Illustrators Internet Home Pages
http://falcon.jmu.edu/~ramseyil/bioyahome.htm

Bantam Doubleday Dell—Teacher's Resource Center
http://www.bdd.com/bin/forums/teachers/index.html

The Internet Public Library—Ask the Author Division
http://www.ipl.org/youth/AskAuthor/

(The biographies listed here also list author home pages where available.)

FOLKTALES FROM AROUND THE WORLD

Aaron Shepard Books

From Russia, Norway, Finland, India, and many other countries, these folktales have been retold by Aaron Shepard. But, once these books are on your shelf of terrific read-alouds, what else can you do with them? Aaron offers some ideas and resources on his Web site.

Author Online!

Aaron Shepard's Home Page

- To find something special, Search Aaron.
- For tips on printing and saving, read Aaron's Help Page.
- To check on changes and additions, see What's New?
- For news about Aaron and his books, look at Flash!
- To contact Aaron, send to AaronShep@aol.com.
- For bulletins by email, subscribe to Aaron's Update.

Welcome! On this page you'll find loads of resources and treats for teachers, librarians, storytellers, children's writers, parents, and young people -- all from award-winning children's author Aaron Shepard. You'll also find info on Aaron, his books, and his author visits. Enjoy!

Visitor count: Over 0052965 for this site.
Site Info | Site Honors

Author Online!—Aaron Shepard's Home Page
http://www.aaronshep.com/

Some of the treats and extras Aaron has included at his Web site are:

- Information about each book, including the country of origin for each folktale.
- Color posters of the landscape and story characters suitable for printing.
- Sound files with word and name pronunciations for those hard-to-pronounce foreign words.
- Sound files with Aaron narrating parts of the folktales.

All of these resources are easily reached by the click of your mouse.

The Baker's Dozen

A Saint Nicholas tale from Dutch colonial America, illustrated by Wendy Edelson. A self-righteous baker gets a lesson in generosity from an old woman and Saint Nicholas. Grades K-7.

- Reader's Theater
- Hear a Portion
- Color Posters
- Other Extras

The Gifts of Wali Dad

A tale of India and Pakistan, illustrated by Daniel San Souci. A humble grasscutter tries again and again to give away unwanted wealth, only to receive ever-greater wealth in return. All ages.

- Reader's Theater
- Hear a Portion
- Color Posters
- Other Extras

The Enchanted Storks

A tale of Bagdad, illustrated by Alisher Dianov. The Calif and his Vizier try a spell that changes them into storks, then find they can't change back. Grades 2 and up.

He has also written and included several Reader's Theater scripts for you to print and use with your students.

The Enchanted Storks
A Tale of Bagdad

Retold by Aaron Shepard

Reader's Theater Edition #6
Version 2.5

Adapted for reader's theater by the author, from *The Enchanted Storks: A Tale of Bagdad*, retold by Aaron Shepard, illustrated by Alisher Dianov, Clarion, New York, 1995

Story and script copyright (c) 1995 Aaron Shepard

"Reader's Theater Editions" is a series of scripts for young readers. The scripts may be freely copied, shared, and performed for any educational, noncommercial purpose. Feel free to format and edit the scripts to serve the needs of your own readers -- but please DO NOT pass on copies with text changes or deletions. All Reader's Theater Editions and supporting materials are posted on the World Wide Web on Aaron's RT Page.

| Aaron Shepard | AaronShep@aol.com | www.aaronshep.com |

GENRE: Fairy tale/folktale

CULTURE: Middle East

THEME: Recklessness

READING LEVEL: Grades 5-9

READERS: 13+

TIME: 14 min.

ROLES: Narrator 1, Narrator 2, Narrator 3, Narrator 4, Calif, Vizier, Khadur, Omar, Princess, Magicians (4), (Guards)

NOTE: This story began as an original fairy tale by the 19th-century German author Wilhelm Hauff in his book *The Caravan*. But it was so popular that it came to be told by storytellers in the Middle East itself. This retelling is based on both original and retold versions. *Calif* is

Use *Web Buddy*'s Site To Go option to download all or part of Aaron's Web site to use with his books.

Tales of Wonder

Another valuable source of folktales from around the world is online at Tales of Wonder.

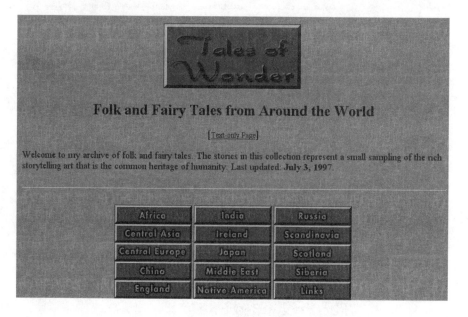

Tales of Wonder
http://darsie.ucdavis.edu/tales/

This award-winning Web site contains a collection of folktales that you can download and use in your classroom.

If you are studying one country, download those stories for students to read and illustrate. You could print the stories and create a bulletin board or wall display with the students' illustrations and a copy of the story.

Use *Web Buddy*'s Conversion option to get a word processed copy of the stories to post.

Older students could choose a story to illustrate and create a book for younger students in your school. If you have a scanner available, you could scan their illustrations and they could create multimedia "books" on the computer using software such as *HyperStudio*®. You could also create Web pages of your own using the stories and scanned illustrations.

Students could use Aaron Shepard's idea of reader's theater scripts. They could create scripts of their own and present skits telling their favorite folktale. Have students work in teams to choose a favorite folktale or to choose one of several from a particular country or region. Each team could represent a different country.

Other Folktale Web Sites:

There are several other Web sites which contain folktales and short stories. You can try these or search online for folktales from a particular country by using "folktales country name" at one of several search engines.

South Uist (Hebrides) Folktales
http://www.hebrides.com/subj/folk.htm

Home Page of Korean Folktales
http://www.csun.edu/~hcedu004/

Creation Stories and Traditional Wisdom
http://www.ozemail.com.au/~reed/global/mythstor.html

Mayan Folktales
http://www.folkart.com/~latitude/folktale/folktale.htm

Japanese Folktales
http://www.arts.unimelb.edu.au/fcf/ucr/student/1996/a.lin/index.html

HAIKU

Haiku is a traditional form of Japanese poetry, usually composed of 3 lines of 5, 7, and 5 syllables, each. Contemporary haiku is not as restrictive and allows 1–3 lines and 17 syllables or less (often 14).

Access through the Internet to countries around the world gives us access to original haiku from as far away as its home country, Japan. What better way to illustrate your study of a Japanese form of poetry than to show your students poetry which came directly from Japan?

Kim's Haiku World

This Web site is one example of a collection of Japanese haiku. The "jp" in the URL signifies that this Web site is actually located on a computer in Japan.

Kim's Haiku

Spring

Summer

Autumn

Winter

Kim's Haiku World
http://cc.matsuyama-u.ac.jp/~shiki/kim/kim.html

As her index indicates, much of the traditional haiku which is written has some reference to the seasons of the year. It is sometimes a subtle reference and the haiku does not need to have the name of the season in it.

Spring

- for ten springs
  to the stars saying nothing
  I have been talking

- cherry blossoms on the hill
  a bell rang
  at the temple

- ah, cherry blossoms
  I wish I could fall
  like you

- perfume of ume blossoms
  my ear lobe
  remembers you

 Quite often the poems are about nature and the descriptions of the scene usually let the reader know what the season is. You are invited to write to Kim and let her know about your own haiku endeavors. You may want to download her haiku as examples using the Site To Go utility and then have your students write haiku to send to her.

Haiku Habitat

haiku habitat

Haiku is about sharp observation and minimalist description. Haiku can transport you to a moment in another time, another place, and put you briefly in contact with another person while they take a deep breath of life. The haiku habitat is a place for me to share with you some of my own haiku, information about haiku and haiku books, and some links off to other nice haiku sites.

Haiku Definitions

definitions of common haiku terms...haiku, tanka, renga, scifaiku, and more...

Spring Puddles

a brief selection of my haiku...both light-hearted and serious...take a little time to splash around in the rain...

Christmas Haiku

someone asked me if I knew of any Christmas haiku, and I didn't...so I tried my hand at it...

Haiku Habitat
© 1996 Tom Brinck
http://www.crew.umich.edu/~brinck/poetry/haikuhabitat.html

Haiku Habitat has much to offer in helping you teach your students how to write haiku. Tom Brinck has created this site to share information about the various forms of haiku. He shares his own haiku with you and also provides many links to other sources of haiku and related poetry on the Internet.

He describes these forms:

- haiku
- scifaiku
- tanka
- waka
- renga
- haikai no renga
- senryu
- haibun
- haiga

 You could download this information, using the Page To Go utility, as a guide as you explain the various forms. Then have these pages available for your students as reminders of the instructions for each form.

Kids Web Japan

Your students can also learn about Japan at another Web site which is actually in Japan.

Kids Web Japan has information which is being provided for students all over the world. The topics include:

- nature and climate
- international relations
- schools, daily life, and sports
- regions of Japan
- economy and industry
- politics and constitution

 If you downloaded this information using the Site To Go utility, you would have a wonderful resource for student lessons about Japan. You could also use the Question and Answer sections of each topic as guidelines for student research or as questions you would like the students to answer as they use this Web site on your computer.

Kids Web Japan
http://www.jinjapan.org/kidsweb/index.html

The Regions of Japan section has a "clickable" map of Japan with links to pages with a more detailed map of each region and a link to more information about that region.

It is within the Tradition and Culture section that you will find the answer to the question, "How do you write a haiku?" They describe haiku as a form of poetry that is about 400 years old.

Other Haiku Web Sites:

Reflections—A Haiku Diary
http://home.pacific.net.sg/~loudon/reflections.htm

A Haiku Homepage
http://www.dmu.ac.uk/~pka/haiku.html

Dhugal J. Lindsay's Haiku Universe
http://www.ori.u-tokyo.ac.jp/~dhugal/haikuhome.html
(extensive information about how to write haiku)

Pizzaz!—Haiku Poems
http://darkwing.uoregon.edu/~leslieob/haiku.html

FROM PHOTOS TO STORIES

It happened again. You gave your students an assignment to write a paragraph or story and they can't think of anything to write about. Try having them pick a photograph to describe. Once they see an image, they can usually find their imaginations and create entire scenarios to accompany it.

Story Starters

This Web site has an assortment of photographs for students to look at. You can use the Site To Go utility to download the pages and the connected digital images.

Story Starters are photographs which can be used by students as subjects for stories or poems. These photographs are all in thumbnail (reduced size) form on this page. Click on a thumbnail to see the normal size graphic.

These photos can be downloaded by teachers for use in their classes without asking for special permission. Use an offline browser, such as Web Buddy, to download this page and the next level of graphics.

Story Starters
http://www.geocities.com/Athens/1573/activities/story1.html

Once you have downloaded the images to disk, your students can use them in word processed documents to illustrate their paragraphs or stories. Ask them to describe what is happening in the photos. Have them tell about what they think the people in some of the photos are doing.

You are invited to send student work to the email address listed on the Web page and it will be posted. Make sure you have some standard for parental permission for student work to be posted on the Internet.

Besides being used to stimulate creativity for stories, these photos can also be used as subject matter for descriptive paragraphs. You can print a photograph on deskjet or inkjet transparency film (be sure to use special transparency film and set your printer for printing on transparencies). Show it to the entire class and have each student describe the scene. This will give them practice in elaborating on descriptions while they have a scene in front of them.

American Memory

This Web site, part of the Library of Congress holdings, has historic photographs which can be used for educational purposes. Some of the photos date back to the early 1800's and are about such varied subjects as California Folk Music, the Civil War, and panoramic views of scenery.

American Memory—Library of Congress
Photographs, Prints & Drawings
http://lcWeb2.loc.gov/ammem/amhome.html

You can download some of those photographs using the Page To Go utility as you find ones which would be useful with this activity.

Some of these photographs could be used in your Social Studies lessons, as well. There are many collections online which could enhance your explanation of historic events.

Other Photograph Web Sites:

Some of these sites have photographs online for educational use, but it would still be a good idea to write to the Webmasters and ask permission prior to using them.

Bill Wright—Fine Art Photographer
http://www.wrightworld.com/

Avishai's Collection of Antique Photographs
http://www.amug.org/~avishai/moreoldphoto.html

Center for Creative Photography
Teacher's Guide for the Exhibition
**http://dizzy.library.arizona.edu/branches/ccp/sisyavgd/
tchguid.htm**

Photos of Silent Era Performers and Artisans
http://www.mdle.com/ClassicFilms/PhotoGallery/index1.htm

The Travel Channel Online Network—Photo Gallery
http://www.travelchannel.com/photo/gallery.htm

Archive Films/Archive Photos Stock Photos and Footage
http://www.archivefilms.com/

Eagle Stock Images—Wildlife Photos
http://www.eaglestock.com/index.htm

LITERATURE AND VIRTUAL MUSEUM TOURS

In *From the Mixed Up Files of Mrs. Basil E. Frankweiler* by E. L. Konigsburg, Claudia and Jamie run away from home. They don't just run down the street; they run away to somewhere special, the Metropolitan Museum of Art in New York City. With the help of the Internet and the museum's online art gallery, you can take your students on a virtual tour of the museum while they are reading this book.

SCORE—CyberGuide

Teacher Guide

From the Mixed-up Files of Mrs. Basil E. Frankweiler

by E. L. Konigsburg

http://www.sdcoe.k12.ca.us/score/tris/tristg.html
CyberGuide by Jean Gahr and Linda Scott
Please forward your comments to the project directu·

SCORE Teacher Guide—CyberGuide
From the Mixed Up Files of Mrs. Basil E. Frankweiler
http://www.sdcoe.k12.ca.us/score/fris/fristg.htm

This is one of the CyberGuides which is part of the SDCOE—San Diego County Office of Education's SCORE (Schools of California Online Resources for Education). You can use the Site To Go utility to download this lesson plan and its associated graphic organizers.

There are graphic organizers available at this Web site to help your students organize their thinking about the book. This Venn Diagram organizer is used in this lesson to study the similarities and differences between Claudia and Jamie. The students are then asked to use the information they filled in the graphic organizer to write compare/contrast paragraphs.

Venn Diagram

The Venn Diagram is made up of two or more overlapping circles. It is often used in mathematics to show relationships between sets. In language arts instruction, Venn Diagrams are useful for examining similarities and differences in characters, stories, poems, etc.

It is frequently used as a prewriting activity to enable students to organize thoughts or textual quotations prior to writing a compare/contrast essay. This activity enables students to organize similarities and differences visually.

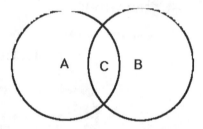

Return to main organizers page or return to main strategies page

Teacher View

The Houghton Mifflin, Co. maintains a section of their Eduplace Web site called Teacher Views. These are a collection of lesson plans, book reviews, and activities written by teachers and submitted to be posted on the Web site and shared by other teachers.

This Teacher View is written about *From the Mixed Up Files of Mrs. Basil E. Frankweiler.*

A visit to the Metropolitan Museum's Online exhibit is also suggested in this guide. This class even went online to a map-generating Web site and requested a close-up map of the area surrounding the museum so they could trace Claudia and Jamie's daily paths.

You can use the Page To Go utility to download this Teacher View lesson plan or use the Site To Go utility to download several and read through them at a later time to choose books for your class to read.

From the Mixed-Up Files of Mrs. Basil E. Frankweiler
by E. L. Konigsburg
Reading Level: 6
Read Aloud Level: 5

TeacherView by Sylvia D. Williams
Grades taught: K, 6
Nashua Elementary School
Nashua, Iowa USA

The Review
This novel is a wonderfully complicated story told by Mrs. Basil E. Frankweiler to her lawyer, Saxonberg. Students can easily relate to the feelings and emotions of Claudia and Jamie who are disillusioned with their parents and have decided to run away from home. Claudia Kincaid has designed a plan for hiding out in the Metropolitan Museum of Art until it is time to return home. The plan becomes complicated when Claudia discovers a beautiful statue that is on display in the museum. She is determined to find out if the statue is the authentic work of Michelangelo. Mrs. Basil E. Frankweiler holds the answer to this puzzle. In addition, she has more surprises for the two youngsters in the last chapter of the book.

The Activity
The setting of this story offers a tremendous opportunity for students to explore New York City and The Metropolitan Museum of Art. I encourage students to use Mapquest

Teacher View
Copyright © 1997 Houghton Mifflin Company. All Rights Reserved.
http://www.eduplace.com/tview/tviews/williams2.html

The Metropolitan Museum of Art
The museum has a virtual art gallery located at this URL:

Metropolitan Museum of Art—New York City
http://www.metmuseum.org

You could start by using the Page To Go utility to download the Web page with the museum map. By printing that on a deskjet or inkjet overhead transparency, the class could follow Claudia and Jamie on their adventures inside the museum. The Site To Go utility would allow you to download a section of the museum so your students could see the interior and have a better understanding of where the children were living.

Other E. L. Konigsburg Web Sites:

SimonSays.com
http://www.simonsays.com

Kids Zone—Authors & Illustrators
E. L. Konigsburg—interview about the book
http://www.simonsays.com/kidzone/auth/ekonigsburg.html

5R's Trip to Museums of the World
http://www.wiscnet.net/edgar/5rmuseum.htm

AIE
http://whyy.org/aie/

Architecture In Education—Architecture in my Classroom?
(activity about the book & thinking about architecture)
http://whyy.org/aie/olney2.html

Other Virtual Art Museum Web Sites:

National Museum of American Art
http://www.nmaa.si.edu/

WebMuseum
http://sunsite.unc.edu/wm/

The Andy Warhol Museum Home Page
http://www.warhol.org/warhol/

Dallas Museum of Art
http://www.unt.edu/dfw/dma/www/dma.htm

Phoenix Art Museum
http://www.azcentral.com/community/phxart/home.html

Birmingham Museum of Art
http://www.hansonlib.org/index.html

TEACHER VIEWS

Teacher Views Literature Lessons for K–8

 Calling all K-8 teachers to write
TeacherViews, reviews and activities for your
favorite classroom books. Submit them to us,
and we'll post them for other teachers around
the world to enjoy and use in their classrooms!

Teacher Mini-Biographies   Submit a TeacherView

TeacherView Postings

- Grade K   - Grade 1   - Grade 2
- Grade 3   - Grade 4   - Grade 5
- Grade 6   - Grade 7   - Grade 8

Teacher Views
http://www.eduplace.com/tview/index.html
Copyright c 1997 Houghton Mifflin Company. All Rights Reserved.

Created by teachers like you and submitted to Houghton Mifflin, Co. for inclusion on this Web site, these are reviews and activities for your favorite classroom books.

Once you have read through the submission guidelines, Houghton Mifflin will invite you to send in your own Teacher View.

The site is a valuable teaching resource. Divided into grade levels for readability, teachers' lesson ideas and activity instructions are online for you to use in your own classrooms.

 **Grade 2 TeacherViews**

The books listed below have a Grade 2 reading level, according to the teachers who submitted the TeacherViews for them. Click on a book title below to read a TeacherView for that book

Matthew's Dream
by Leo Lionni

The Library
by Sarah Stewart

The Paper Bag Princess
by Robert Munsch

What's So Terrible About Swallowing an Apple Seed?
by Harriet Lerner and Susan Goldhor

I Get the Creeps
by Sharon Siamon

Where the Wild Things Are

Grade 2 Index
Copyright © 1997 Houghton Mifflin Company. All Rights Reserved.

 Choose the grade level you teach (or suggest to your librarian or media specialist that they download them all) and use the Site To Go option to download all the activities online.

Later, you can read through them and choose the next book you want to use with your students. The activities are already described for you. The teacher who wrote the activity has designated the reading level for students reading the book on their own as well as a read-aloud reading level in case you plan to read the book to your students.

There is a Review section of the Teacher View in which the teacher gives you some background or a summary of the book.

The main section of the Teacher View is the Activity section. Here the teacher describes activities he or she has done with students in the past. Materials needed are listed and any preparations you need to make in advance are given. Student instructions are also explained.

 If you only needed a Teacher View for one book, you could use the Page To Go utility to download just that page.

Where the Wild Things Are
by Maurice Sendak
Reading Level: 2
Read Aloud Level: Kindergarten

TeacherView by Laura Hoyler
Grade taught: 3
Dominion Trail Elementary
Ashburn, Virginia USA

The Review

Where the Wild Things Are is the classic tale of young Max who is sent to bed without supper. Max then dreams that he is in the land of the wild things, and is king. But Max misses his home, so he sails back, and finds dinner waiting for him!

The Activity

1. Provide each student with a long legal size paper. You can use legal size copy paper or thicker art paper if you wish. Have the students fold their paper into thirds. (The paper should be facing the direction you would write on it, up and down, not side to side.)

2. Have each student draw a large monster head in the top rectangle of the paper, staying only in the top section. When they are done, have them pass their paper to another student and have the

This is a Teacher View for *Where the Wild Things Are* aimed at 2nd Grade students.

Tuck Everlasting
by Natalie Babbitt
Reading Level: 5
Read Aloud Level: 5

TeacherView by Kimberly Lojas
Grades taught: 5
St. John Fisher
Chicago, Illinois USA

The Review

This book opens wonderful doors of discussion for any class. *Tuck Everlasting* tells the story of a little girl named Winnie Foster who experiences some unique events.

Winnie comes from a small Southern town and a prestigious family. However, Winnie's life takes a drastic turn when she meets the Tucks. The Tucks have discovered a fountain in the middle of the woods. If a person drinks from it, that person can live forever, regardless of what they do. They can shoot themselves, fall from trees and other fatal activities.

Winnie stumbles onto a boy drinking from the fountain--the youngest Tuck. The boy takes her to meet the other Tucks, and Winnie must decide whether she wants to join the Tucks, as they live forever

This book is beautifully written with language that not only sets the mood, but also introduces

The teacher who wrote this Teacher View for *Tuck Everlasting* explained that she read the book aloud to her 5th Grade students and discussed parts of it as she read it. Then she explains activities she had her students do before finishing the book.

CYBERGUIDES

Teacher Guides and Student Activities

The CyberGuides Web site is maintained by the San Diego County Office of Education as a part of SCORE (Schools of California Online Resources for Education). The teacher guides and activities are created by teachers to lead students in online activities that correlate with pieces of literature they are reading.

They are part of the Language Arts Resources Web site at this URL:

http://www.sdcoe.k12.ca.us/score/cla.html

Teacher Guides & Student Activities

CyberGuides are supplementary units of instruction based on core works of literature, designed for students to use the World Wide Web. Most guides are not designed as comprehensive units but as collections of Web-searching activities that lead to a student product. They are designed for the classroom with one computer, connected to the Internet.

Each CyberGuide contains:
- a student and teacher edition
- a statement of objectives
- a task and a process by which it may be completed
- a rubric for assessing the quality of the product

Honored by:

We encourage you to try the CyberGuide of your choice, fieldtest it and send us your response. Send your comments to Don Mayfield or Linda Taggart-Fregoso, Coordinators, SCORE Language Arts Project.

CyberGuides
http://www.sdcoe.k12.ca.us/score/cyberguide.html

This format would work for Web sites that you had downloaded onto your computer's hard drive, as well. You would need to enter the file name and directory/folder location where it resides on disk.

The format for a CyberGuide includes:

> a student and teacher edition
> a statement of objectives
> a task and a process by which it may be completed
> a rubric for assessing the quality of the product

The Web site index is divided into grades K–3, 4–5, 6–8, and 9–12 reading levels. You could download and use any or all of the guides that are already online. The teachers who created them would be happy to hear from you.

Grades K-3	Grades 6-8	Grades 9-12
Annie and the Old One by Miska Miles	Adam of the Road by Elizabeth Janet Gray	The Adventures of Huckleberry Finn by Mark Twain
Apples (A Thematic Unit)	Aztec Legends	The Buck Private by Luis Valdez
Dear Mr. Blueberry by Simon James	Canyons by Gary Paulsen	Chicano Literature: I am Joaquin by Corky Gonzalez
The Desert is Theirs by Byrd Baylor	Catherine Called Birdie by Karen Cushman	The Crucible by Arthur Miller
Frog and Toad Are Friends by Arnold Lobel	Charles Dickens: An Author Unit	
	The Dark Frigate by Charles Boardman Hawes	Cry, the Beloved Country by Alan Paton
How My Parents Learned to Eat by Ina R. Friedman	Dear Mr. Henshaw by Beverly Cleary	Farewell to Manzanar by Jean Houston and James D. Houston
Little House in the Big Woods by Laura Ingalls Wilder	A Day No Pigs Would Die by Robert Peck	
	The Drummer Boy of Shiloh by Ray Bradbury	Their Eyes Were Watching God by Zora Neale Hurston
The Mitten by Janet Brett	The Egypt Game by Elizabeth Keatley Snyder	
My Great Aunt Arizona by Gloria Houston	The Golden Goblet by Eloise Jarvis McGraw	The Legend of Llorona by Rudolfo Anaya
	Harriet Tubman by Ann Petry	Hamlet by William Shakespeare
	Journey to Jo'burg by Beverly Naidoo	

There are templates online for creating the lessons. You only need to download the template file and fill in the information for the book you are studying. You could edit the template file in your browser's edit utility or in a simple text editor. The template shows you how to edit it and gives you instructions for how it should be completed.

The CyberGuides Student Activity Template with HTML guidelines is located here:

http://www.sdcoe.k12.ca.us/score/templates/basicstu.html

Student Activity 2

Students will visit several Web sites and gather information about desert plants, especially the saguaro cactus. They will organize this information in a Learning Log.

Desert USA -Flora
URL: http://www.desertusa.com/flora.html

Desert Images
URL: http://www.goldcanyon.com/htm/images.htm

Saguaro Cactus Close Up
URL: http://eies.njit.edu/~4064/closeup.htm

Student Activity 3

Students will visit several Web sites to learn about the Tohono O'odham (Papago). They will locate their reservation on a map. They will discover that Tohono O'odham means desert people. They will read (or have read to them) the Tohono O'odham creation myth. They should record what they learn in their Learning Log.

Reservation Map
URL: http://thememall.com/tribes/indians.html-ssi
Click on the purple reservation near Arizona's southern border and a brief article about the Papago come. up.

CyberGuide for *The Desert Is Theirs* by Byrd Baylor
Susan D. Murphy

This teacher guide provides information about the instructions for learning about saguaro cactus and the desert people. This is done by asking students to look at some specific Web sites to find answers to questions.

You could download those Web sites with the Site To Go utility and then have the entire activity and connected Web sites on your hard drive or on a zip disk.

Introduction

This supplemental unit to *Blue Willow* was developed as part of the Schools of California OnlineResources for Educators (SCORE) Project, funded by the CaliforniaTechnology Assistance Program (CTAP).

Disclaimer: The links here have been scrutinized for their grade and age appropriateness; however, contents of links on the World Wide Web change continuously. It is advisable that teachers review all links before introducing CyberGuides to students.

This unit, designed to supplement the teaching of Blue Willow by Doris Gates, consists of five activities that address the following five questions, respectively:

1. *What is the impact of the San Joaquin Valley on California and the nation in terms of agriculture?*

2. *What aspects of your California county should be highlighted and displayed in a fair exhibit?*

3. *What is the history of carousels and what animals are commonly represented on carousels?*

4. *How is cotton produced and how are fabrics produced from raw cotton?*

5. *Where is Route 66 and why was it important to California?*

CyberGuide for *Blue Willow* by Doris Gates
Dana Weld

This teacher's guide begins with the introduction, explaining the objectives of the lesson and student activities for this book.

There are corresponding Student Activity Web pages with background information for the student to read and specific questions the teacher wants them to research and answer while visiting the associated Web sites.

The Process: Exploring the Web, Creating a Product

On your California map label the San Joaquin Valley. Visit the web sites to identify crops which are grown in this area. Select a product you are interested in and take notes from the site about this product. You will need to know what this product looks like, how it is grown and how much of it is commonly produced in a year.

After you have completed your research, draw a picture of your crop or print one from the web site. Attach your map and picture to a large piece of paper. Write a paragraph describing this product and attach it under the picture. Draw a line from your picture to the area in the San Joaquin Valley where this product is grown.

Agricultural Web Link
This page will give you information on different crops grown in California. Click on the crop you are interested in

California Agriculture Facts
This page has facts about products grown in California

Fruit Facts
This page focuses on fruits grown in California

California Farm BureauCommodity Fact Sheets
This page has individual links for specific agriculture products grown in California

UC. Fruit and Nut Information and Research Center
Links to pages for information on fruits and nuts, many of which are grown in California.

This is where you would edit the file and include the file name locations for the files you had downloaded to your disk.

These are completed lessons for you to use in your classroom with your own students. You can also follow the format and create CyberGuides of your own. You could also e-mail the author of each CyberGuide you use and tell him or her how you used it and whether you had to adjust it for your class. You could share any CyberGuides you create with some of the teachers on the list who created one for a book by the same author you might choose.

Don Mayfield and Linda Taggart-Fregoso, Coordinators of the SCORE Language Arts Project would like to know when you use the guides. Please let them know by e-mailing them at the address on the index page.

IN THE NEWS

With access to the Internet and the thousands of newspapers that are now online, you can quickly and easily find information for your students about life in different communities, around the country, and even around the world.

This process can be used to illustrate the theme of "community" in the elementary grades. It can also be used in Language Arts and Social Studies classes to teach about reading newspaper articles and about different regions of the United States and the world.

Internet Press

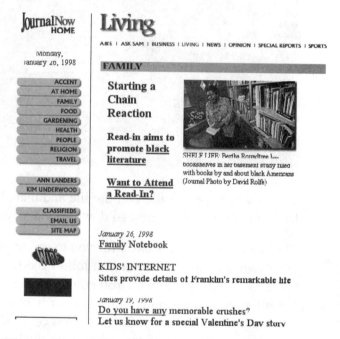

Internet Press
http://gallery.uunet.be/internetpress/

This award-winning Web site provides you with links to news sites worldwide. Listings of each country and state include newspapers, magazines, radio stations, and television stations that have Web sites.

Once you choose the country or state you are studying, click on the hypertext link in Internet Press's list. You will see a list of all the news sources for that location.

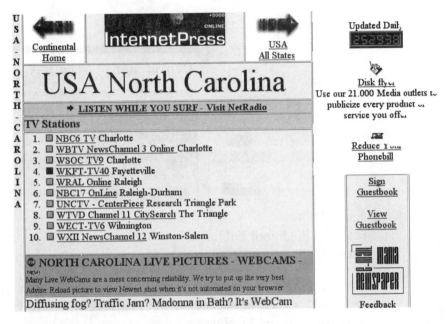

Internet Press—North Carolina
http://www.club.innet.be/~year0230/ncarolin.htm

Each available Web site is linked in a list which is divided according to media type. You simply click on the hypertext link to go to that news source's Web site.

In order to provide information about communities in other states, you could use the Site To Go utility to download several newspapers. Then share them with the class at your classroom computer.

You could also use *Web Buddy*'s Schedule utility to schedule daily downloads of several newspapers. This utility is great for those busy mornings when you can't find the time to sit down at the computer and manually download the materials. *Web Buddy* will dial your Internet provider and download the scheduled newspapers, and all you need to do is save them to disk and take the disk with you to class.

Winston-Salem JournalNow

JournalNow
(c) 1998 Piedmont Publishing
http://www.JournalNow.com/

As an example, if your class is studying North Carolina, you could download several newspapers from that state and have your students look for state and local news.

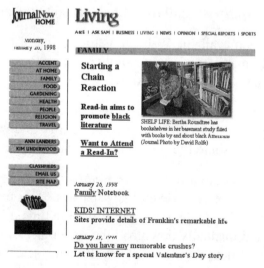

This paper has a Living section which gives information about the local communities.

CyberStar

CyberStar—The Shelby Star Online
http://www.shelbystar.com/

Smaller newspapers focus more on local news. They are a good source of information about communities. Many of them have Web pages about local government, schools, and entertainment.

By finding the community link at each newspaper, you can find all the local information.

You can use newspapers from different states to compare and contrast ways of life, schools, and even the weather at a certain time of year. Have the students look at the photographs in the articles and describe the weather that area is having. Quite often, there is a weather section in the newspaper, as well.

 Some of these newspapers could serve as guidelines for you and your students to create a school or neighborhood online newspaper of your own. You could use digital images (digital or scanned photographs and artwork) to turn your school print newspaper into an online newspaper to have saved on your school's network or on single machines. You could distribute diskettes each week to all the teachers so they could have the newspaper on their computer for students to read.

Internet Press also has links to newspapers in countries around the world. You may not be able to read them all, but your students can still look at the photographs and get a visual impression of that country and its people. They might be surprised to find just how many other countries actually post a newspaper in English.

Other Online Newspaper Education Web Sites:

Teaching Current Events Via Newspapers, Magazines, and TV
http://www.csun.edu/~hcedu013/cevents.html

Newspapers In Education—NIE Online
(lesson plans about using The Detroit News and other online newspapers in your classroom)
http://www.detnews.com/nie/

Newspapers In Education—The Seattle Times Online
http://www.seattletimes.com/nie/

Newspapers In Education—The Fort Worth Star-Telegram Online
http://www.star-traveler.com/today/news/education/nie/index.htm

Newspaper Assignments
http://www.shastalink.k12.ca.us/telementors/news.html

MATH & MOLECULES

MathMol

This Web site illustrates the very real connection between mathematics and science. You'll be able to use these activities with both subjects in the elementary grades. If you teach middle school math, you might want to get the science teacher involved with this unit as well.

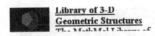 MathMol K-12 Activity Page

---

MathMol (Mathematics and Molecules) is designed to serve as an introductory starting point for K-12 students and teachers interested in the field of molecular modeling and its application to mathematics

---

 MathMol Quick Tour: What is molecular modeling? Why is it so important? What is the relationship between molecules and mathematics?

 **Hypermedia Textbook for Grades 6-12** NEW Visit an experimental textbook of the future that makes full use of the latest in Netscape capabilities, including: frames, VRML, interactive Javascipt files, animated GIF's and MPEG files

 Library of 3-D Geometric Structures The MathMol Library of

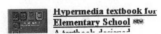 **Hypermedia textbook for Elementary School** NEW A textbook designed

MathMol
http://www.nyu.edu/pages/mathmol/K_12.html

Designed at the New York University Scientific Visualization Center, this Web site uses images, mpeg movie files, and VRML (Virtual Reality Modeling Language) to provide you with an interactive unit about the mathematics of molecular modeling.

You will need an "mpg" movie viewer and VRML viewer to see the movies and work with the 3D manipulative geometric and molecular models. Those can be available with your browser or freeware versions can be downloaded from several sources online.

Quick Tour of MathMol

What is Molecular Modeling?

Molecular Modeling, is one of the fastest growing fields in science. It may vary from building and visualizing molecules (click image below for a short animation)...

...to performing complex calculations on molecular systems. Below, molecular dynamics simulations are performed on a lipid-protein complex. Shown are the backbone structure of the protein, a bound fatty acid molecule within the protein, and a small shell of water surrounding the protein. The time for the simulation was 100 picoseconds. The graphs give information about the motion of the lipid inside the protein

The quick tour provides you with background information about the Web site and molecular modeling with illustrations and animations. Students will see 3D moving models of various molecules and read descriptions of how scientists view the angles within them.

Many molecules have similar shapes to familiar geometric space figures such as hexagons and pentagons. There are VRML files with manipulative space figures—from 2 dimensional plane figures such as pentagons and rectangles to 3 dimensional figures such as columns, cubes, and dodecahedrons.

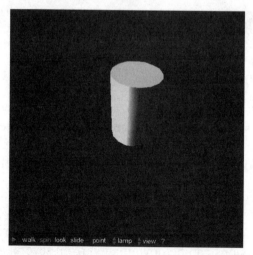

There is a Hypermedia Textbook for Elementary School with lessons about water molecules for grades 3–6 and a Hypermedia Textbook for grades 6–12. It covers every subject from lines and rays to 3 dimensional molecule models. You can use the Site To Go utility to download a textbook or you may just want to download the VRML graphics libraries to illustrate your lesson.

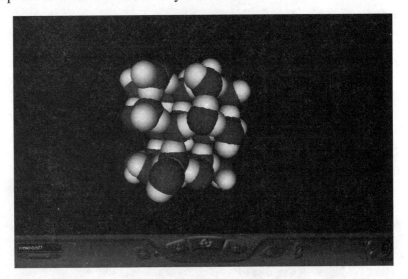

Students can follow the textbook's lessons, view the graphics, watch the movies, work with the models, and answer questions to test their knowledge.

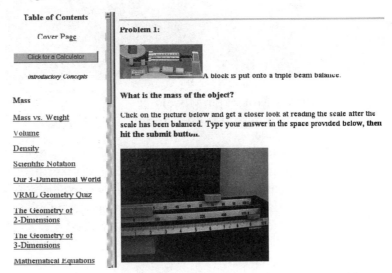

As students are using the "textbook," have them make models of the geometric and molecular figures, too. Younger students can practice by cutting 2-dimensional figures and finding examples of many of the 3-dimensional figures in real life. Older students can create paper models of the 3-dimensional geometric figures and stick-and-ball models of the molecules.

Chemistry Molecular Models

For more examples of 3-dimensional models of molecules, look at this Web site from the chemistry department of the University of Wisconsin—Stevens Point. Dr. Thomas Zamis maintains this Web site of images that you can view with your *Netscape* browser and a plug-in or with a separate program. Both can be downloaded for free from sites linked on the page.

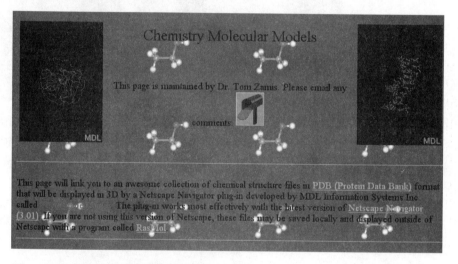

Chemistry Molecular Models
http://chemdept.uwsp.edu/pdbs/

The models are in PDB (Protein DataBase) format. Once you have them open in Netscape, through the plug-in, or in the program, your students can manipulate them and view how each molecule is organized. They can change the options for viewing in order to see them as stick figures or as sticks and balls.

The water molecule shown here can be turned by using the mouse and can be changed back to a thin stick figure so that students can measure the angle of the atoms within the molecule.

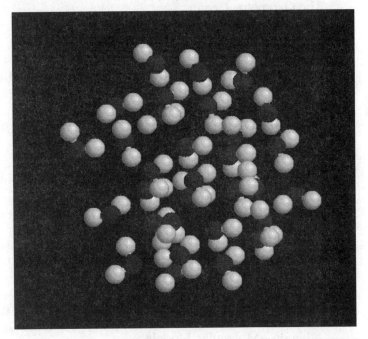

In this view of an ice molecule, students can locate the individual water molecules.

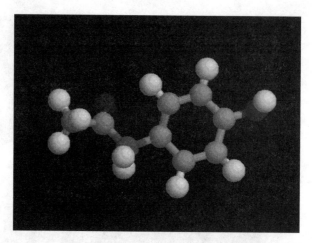

Have students use styrofoam balls or gumdrops and toothpicks to re-create molecules such as this Tylenol molecule. Or have them use the wireframe view and measure the angles of the connections.

Other Geometry Web Sites:

The Geometry Center
http://www.geom.umn.edu/

A Teacher's Guide to Building the Icosahedron as a Class Project
http://www.geom.umn.edu/docs/education/build-icos/

Math Forum—K–12 Geometry
http://forum.swarthmore.edu/geometry/k12.geometry.html

The Geometry Junkyard
http://www.ics.uci.edu/~eppstein/junkyard/topic.html

Other Molecular Modeling Web Sites:

The Chemistry of Carbon
http://www.nyu.edu/pages/mathmol/modules/carbon/carbon1.html

Assembling the Methane Molecule
http://www.eosc.osshe.edu/chemWeb/molmodel/mmp9c.html

Athenor—Molecular Models
http://ourworld.compuserve.com/homepages/JDebord/models.htm

MATHEMATICAL THINKING

MegaMath

The MegaMath Workbook is a project created by a group of teachers, scientists, mathematicians, and students. It was completed by the Computer Research and Applications Group at Los Alamos National Laboratory.

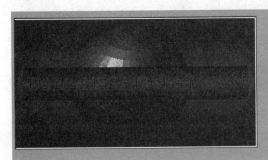

Introducing MegaMath

Mathematics is a live science with new discoveries being made every day. The frontier of mathematics is an exciting place, where mathematicians experiment and play with creative and imaginative ideas. Many of these ideas are accessible to young children. Others (infinity is a good example) are ideas that have already piqued many children's curiosity, but their profound mathematical importance is not widely known or understood. The MegaMath project is intended to bring unusual and important mathematical ideas to elementary school classrooms so that young people and their teachers can think about them together.

MegaMath
© 1993 Nancy Casey
http://www.c3.lanl.gov/mega-math/welcome.html

The lessons are based on questions that you and your students can work together to solve. They involve hands-on exploratory activities and having students practice their mathematical thinking, problem-solving, and communication skills.

The topics chosen are current mathematical problems. You will be presenting your students with a problem they can concentrate on solving. In the words of the authors, "We will have succeeded if you, and the children in your care, enjoy the stories and activities and come away from them with some annoying unanswered questions."

Learn My Language

Description

Students act out the operation of a <u>finite state machine</u> that has been drawn with masking tape on the classroom floor. Students receive (or make) tickets that serve as inputs to the machine. The tickets tell them which lines on the floor to follow and which circles or <u>states</u> to pass through. If they end up in an <u>accept state</u> they receive a prize. This means that what was printed on their ticket was recognized by the machine as a <u>word</u> in its <u>language</u> .

▪ Materials

▪ Instructions

▪ Ideas for discussion

▪ For further Investigation

Materials

- Finite State Machine drawn on the floor as described <u>below</u>.
- For each student:
  - Several strips of paper, approximately 2" X 8".

One of the activities, called "Learn My Language," is part of the topic "Machines That Eat Your Words." This topic is about finite state machines. These are abstract machines that are used to design systems to identify patterns.

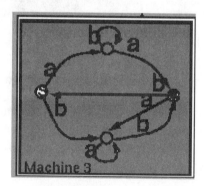

In this activity, you and your students will be creating a finite state machine to solve the problem of what words belong in a certain machine's language. You will create this "machine" with masking tape on the floor and the students will walk through the activity following some instructions given.

Each topic has the following components: Background Information, Prep & Materials, Vocabulary, Big Ideas & Key Concepts, Activities, Evaluation, and Further Study.

The topics have several activities to explain the concept being discussed. Sometimes there are variations included for students of different age ranges.

 You will probably want to use the Site To Go utility to download all the materials for one topic and keep them handy on your computer. This is especially helpful with some pages which have large graphics for you to print.

Overview

Sometimes we don't think we have enough information to solve a problem, but in reality we do. We can use logical analysis to pin down information which, although not explicitly stated, can be inferred from what we know.

Students perform a <u>play</u> which takes place in a school where some of the students always lie and the rest always tell the truth. Terry, the protagonist, is trying to find out which students are which, but at the beginning, there is no way of knowing whom to believe.

At first it seems like there is never enough information, but in each case, it is possible for Terry figure out more about the students that might have seemed possible.

Another lesson focuses on the idea that quite often it seems that you don't have enough information to solve a problem but with careful thinking, you can eventually find the solution. The story presented in "Just a Usual Day at Unusual School" is an example of one of those problems.

Let the MegaMath team know how you and your students enjoyed working with the problems. Their e-mail address is on the Web pages and they invite feedback from classes using the materials.

MATH TABLES & FORMULAS

Have you ever searched for that one elusive math table? Or have you ever wanted to post all the formulas for calculating area or volume on your bulletin board but been unable to find them?

Dave's Math Tables

Dave's Math Tables Web site is just the answer. From general math to statistics and calculus, David Manura has compiled a collection of tables and formulas for a variety of needs.

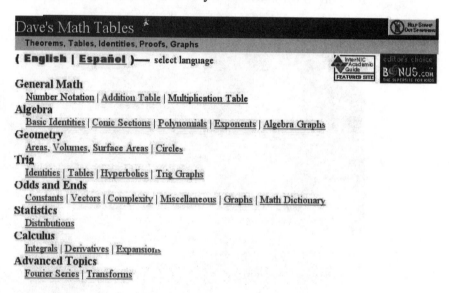

Dave's Math Tables
http://www.sisWeb.com/math/tables.htm

You could use the Site To Go utility to download his entire site to your computer's hard drive or to a zip disk to take with you to school.

This will be a valuable resource for students to be able to use whenever they are trying to solve a particular problem and can't find the correct formula.

You could also use the Page To Go utility if you only needed one of the pages for a particular concept you were teaching.

You will find addition and multiplication tables suitable for printing. Although these tables are not suitable for *Web Buddy*'s Convert utility, you will be able to print them from your downloaded Web page.

Dave's Math Tables: *Multiplication Table* UP

(Math | General | **MultiplicationTable**)

Multiplication Table

x	0	1	2	3	4	5	6	7	8	9	10	11	12
0	0	0	0	0	0	0	0	0	0	0	0	0	0
1	0	1	2	3	4	5	6	7	8	9	10	11	12
2	0	2	4	6	8	10	12	14	16	18	20	22	24
3	0	3	6	9	12	15	18	21	24	27	30	33	36
4	0	4	8	12	16	20	24	28	32	36	40	44	48
5	0	5	10	15	20	25	30	35	40	45	50	55	60
6	0	6	12	18	24	30	36	42	48	54	60	66	72
7	0	7	14	21	28	35	42	49	56	63	70	77	84
8	0	8	16	24	32	40	48	56	64	72	80	88	96
9	0	9	18	27	36	45	54	63	72	81	90	99	108

There are diagrams for formulas where appropriate so your students will be able to visualize the formula reference as well.

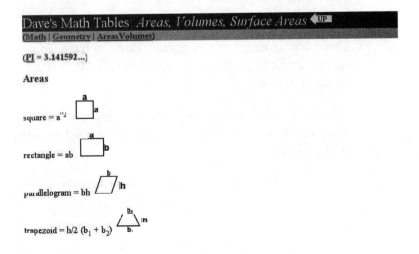

Dave's Math Tables: *Areas, Volumes, Surface Areas* UP

(Math | Geometry | **AreasVolumes**)

($\underline{PI}$ = 3.141592...)

Areas

square = a^2

rectangle = ab

parallelogram = bh

trapezoid = $h/2 \, (b_1 + b_2)$

PUZZLING MATH CONCEPTS

The Little Math Puzzle Contest

Puzzles about math—this site is full of them. Created and maintained by Tom Murray and his students at Royal West Academy in Montréal, Quebec, Canada, this site posts a new math puzzle each week for your students to attempt to solve.

About the Little Math Puzzle | Archives | Winner's List | The Current Puzzle

Interactive Archives of the 95/96 puzzles #1-37.
Your Browser must be frames & Java capable (Netscape 3)

The Little Math Puzzle Contest

These are weekly puzzles posted to the SchoolNet Listserv. This activity is intended to be an internet icebreaker activity for a wide range of classrooms across Canada. Hopefully, it is something we can all do together as we start to explore the possibilities of internet before we start more involved projects.
This project is best followed through the SchoolNet listserv send a message to **listproc@schoolnet.ca** saying **subscribe schoolnet your name**.

Royal West Academy students have shared the responsibility of posting the problems and creating the Winner's Lists. We are all greatly appreciative of their efforts.

Kate

The **answers** are available if you have the password. answers The Password will be shared with teachers through a written request. Send a request to *math_puzzle@rwa.psbgm.qc.ca*

The Little Math Puzzle Contest
http://www.microtec.net/~academy/mathpuzzle

There are sequencing and pattern puzzles from Tom and his students as well as from students at other schools. This is a great weekly thinking activity.

In order to get the answers to the puzzles, you must send an email to this address and let them know you are a teacher using the puzzles in your classroom:

math_puzzle@rwa.psbgm.qc.ca

WELCOME TO PROBLEM #218

VOILA LE PROBLEME #218

"We seek order and pattern in all things and sometimes change our paradigm."

"Nous cherchons l'ordre dans tout et quelques fois, nous changeons notre approche"

Here is how to submit your answer in 3 easy steps:

Donnez votre réponse comme suit

Step I

Examine the following set of numbers:

Étape I

Analysez les nombres suivants

	62	60	30	32	64	62	31	33	66	64	32	34	68	

Step II

Determine the missing numbers.

Étape II

Completez la serie avec les nombres manquants.

Step III

Fill out the information below and submit it to The Little Math Puzzle.

Étape III

Donnez l'information demandée ci-dessous et soumettez-la

Your name/Votre nom

Each week's puzzle is posted at this URL:

http://www.microtec.net/~academy/mathpuzzle/currentpuzzle.html

Since the Web site is located in Montréal, the puzzles are also posted in French. If your students are learning French in your elementary or middle school, you might want to share this site with the French teacher, as well. It would be a great way to reinforce their language skills.

You can schedule *Web Buddy* to download this site on a weekly basis so you don't forget to do it and you don't have to post notes on your computer monitor to help you remember. The Scheduling utility can be set to download a page on the same day and time each week. You can also set your scheduling preferences to let you know when you miss a scheduled download in case your computer was off at that time.

The Web site also has an archive of the past years' puzzles. You can use the Site To Go utility to download those pages and spend time teaching your students how to solve them or have special classroom contests.

```
Puzzle 201 ********************************************************
What meaning can you find in the following?
          ( set your e-mail reader to courier )

                    F   N   H   L   N   L   R   D
                    I   T   O   O   E   O
                    D   S   I   T   W
                    E   T   D   E
                    U   N   H
                    A   T
                    L
                    L

Puzzle 202 ********************************************************
What is the next number in this pattern?

          2, 2, 2, 6, 10, 18, 34, 62, 114, _____

Puzzle 203 ********************************************************
What is the single letter solution in this closed sequence?

A, F, S, N, I, S, R, M, E, Q, W, B, S, D, N, Z, A, C, E, D, H, C, T

Puzzle 204 ********************************************************
What is the next number in this open sequence?

          1, 3, 6, 9, 27, 31, 124, 129, __

Puzzle 205 ********************************************************
What are the two letters that complete this set?

O, Z, W, X, E,    , R, V, T, B, Y, N,    , M.
```

If you want to use these as worksheets for your students, you can
print the files from your browser so the puzzles like the one above
look correct.

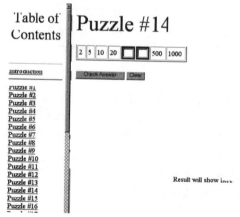

There is also an interactive archive of the 1995–1996 puzzles. Your

students can use these puzzles as independent activities on your
computer once you have used the Site To Go utility to download
them. If they key in the correct answer, the screen at the bottom will
show that. If not, they get a message to try again.

Geometry Problem of the Week

This is another weekly puzzle site with puzzles about Geometry concepts. It is part of the Math Forum Web site. You can schedule *Web Buddy* to download this every Monday morning and the students have all week to attempt to solve it and to submit answers to the sponsors. They will respond with hints for solving if the students are incorrect.

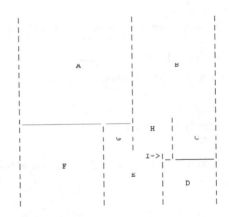

Geometry
Problem of the Week

Submit Your Solution   Last Solution   The Archives
Rules   Help for Teachers   Help for Students   Recognition & Awards
Project of the Month   Student Center   Teachers' Place

Making a Quilt of Squares
January 12-16, 1998

I am thinking of making a quilt from an illustration that appeared on the cover of Scientific American magazine a while ago. I need some helping figuring a few things out, though.

The picture below illustrates the problem. All I know is that all of the pieces are squares, and that the area of C is 64 square inches and the area of D is 81 square inches. Here's what I need to know.

Will the finished shape be a square? If I want to quilt along all of the lines (including the outside edge), how much thread will I need? (Assume that it takes 1.5 inches of thread to quilt 1 inch of the line.)

Geometry Puzzle of the Week
http://forum.swarthmore.edu/geopow/

These puzzles are geared toward older students, but many middle school students may enjoy the challenge. Solutions are usually posted by the end of the following week.

Other Math Puzzles Web Sites:

Math Problems & Puzzles
http://forum.swarthmore.edu/~steve/steve/mathpuzzles.html

Casio Classroom Puzzle of the Week
http://pegasus.cc.ucf.edu/~mathed/problem.html
- Elementary Brain Teaser
- Middle School Madness

(names of correct students will be posted on the Web page and a drawing is held from that group of students to award a Casio calculator)

Casio Classroom (calculator lessons sent in by other teachers)
http://pegasus.cc.ucf.edu/~ucfcasio/casio.htm

ABsurd MAth
http://www.hrmvideo.com/abmath/index.html

Word Problems for Kids (Grades 5–12)
http://juliet.stfx.ca/people/fac/pwang/mathpage/math1.html

Math Puzzles
http://www.searnet.com/~dedwards/math.htm

Mr. Finch's Class
http://www.mbnet.mb.ca/~jfinch/

Finch Math Problems of the Week
(schedule *Web Buddy* to download these at the beginning of each month)
http://www.mbnet.mb.ca/~jfinch/math.html

PIGS IN CYBERSPACE

PIGS Space—Cooperative Networking Website

Maintained by the PIGS Team of administrators and teachers in New Brunswick, Canada, this Web site contains lesson plans for a variety of subjects. The lesson plans all involve the following four elements of cooperative learning:

P = Positive Interdependence
I = Individual Accountability
G = Group Processing
S = Social Interaction

PIGS in Cyberspace
http://cspace.unb.ca/nbco/pigs/

This team consists of six educators who have studied David and Roger Johnson's philosophy of "Cooperation in the Classroom." This use of the Internet certainly shows that these 4 basic components of cooperation can exist not only with face-to-face encounters within your classroom walls but also via Internet communication with classes in other parts of your country or the World.

This Web site contains lessons created by New Brunswick teachers. They relate to the New Brunswick Curriculum, but can be used with almost any curriculum. Where appropriate, the teachers have also included enrichment activities within the classroom and Internet activities between cooperating classrooms.

Modules: Writing

Title: Descriptive Paragraphs: Artistic Impressions

Author: District 16 Cooperative Networking Team, Miramichi, N.B.

Subject: Language Arts

Grade level: 4-8

Objectives :
To have students write descriptive paragraphs which contain detailed descriptions, highlighted by specific moods.

Cooperative Methods:
Students will work in pairs. One student will write a descriptive paragraph of any room in his/her home. Their partner, using the descriptive paragraph, will illustrate the room.

Student Examples:

Steven Scott: My Sister's Room
I'm sitting on my sister's bed where she used to sleep. Across from that high-backed chair is her closet that looks like it has never been opened. It reminds me of King Tut's tomb. Her books, lined up in rows on her bookshelves, are waiting to be read. Her window is shut tight so no light can get through until ..... my sister comes home from

Descriptive Paragraphs: Artistic Impressions
http://cspace.unb.ca/nbco/pigs/writing/write2.html

This writing lesson is an example of the lesson plans you will find at the site. You can download these lesson plans by using the Site To Go utility or, if you only need one, you can use the Convert utility and save it as a word processing file to use as you create the instructions for your students.

This plan also suggests a cooperative activity with another class via the Internet. The original activity has students work in pairs. Each student describes a room in his or her house. Then students switch papers and illustrate the room in the paragraph. An e-mail activity with another class could have those students send the paragraphs via e-mail to students in another school. The students who receive the e-mail can use the computer to do illustrations of the rooms and then e-mail the graphics back.

Another extension of that activity might be to create a Web site of your own and post the paragraphs and illustrations online for both classes to share.

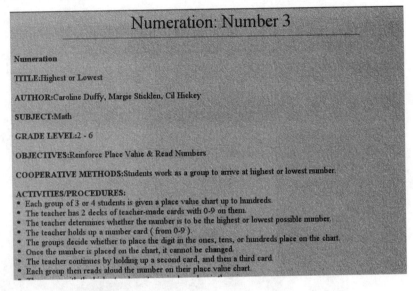

Numeration: Number 3

Numeration

TITLE: Highest or Lowest

AUTHOR: Caroline Duffy, Margie Sticklen, Cil Hickey

SUBJECT: Math

GRADE LEVEL:2 - 6

OBJECTIVES: Reinforce Place Value & Read Numbers

COOPERATIVE METHODS: Students work as a group to arrive at highest or lowest number.

ACTIVITIES/PROCEDURES:
* Each group of 3 or 4 students is given a place value chart up to hundreds.
* The teacher has 2 decks of teacher-made cards with 0-9 on them.
* The teacher determines whether the number is to be the highest or lowest possible number.
* The teacher holds up a number card (from 0-9).
* The groups decide whether to place the digit in the ones, tens, or hundreds place on the chart.
* Once the number is placed on the chart, it cannot be changed.
* The teacher continues by holding up a second card, and then a third card.
* Each group then reads aloud the number on their place value chart.

Highest or Lowest

Another lesson online at the PIGS Web site is a math lesson about learning place value and reading numbers.

You could use the Site To Go utility to download all the lesson plans online at this time, but you should visit the site often since other teachers will be contributing new lessons periodically. You might also like to share a lesson of your own with them. There is a template online which shows how they want the lesson plans written and submitted.

At this time, they have lessons in a variety of categories including Reading, Writing, Listening and Speaking, Numeration, Operations, Measurement, Geometry, Inventions, Our Environment, and Community.

They are also interested in how you are using the lessons in your classroom, so feel free to send them an e-mail and let them know how you enjoyed using the lessons or how you adapted them to fit your curriculum.

GEORGE WASHINGTON & MOUNT VERNON

How much do you and your students really know about George Washington and his home, Mount Vernon? Did George Washington really chop down a cherry tree? Did he really have false teeth made of wood?

This Web site, with its historical information and lesson materials, provides you with all the materials you need to teach your students the answers to these and many other questions.

Historic Mount Vernon

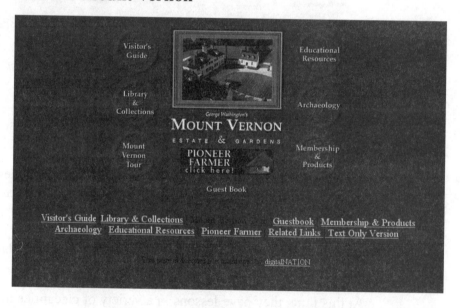

Historic Mount Vernon—The Home of our First President
http://www.mountvernon.org

The opening screen leads you to the Mount Vernon Tour and Educational Resources which tell the story of the Mount Vernon estate and George Washington's life.

MOUNT VERNON
GROUNDS TOUR

Study

George Washington had this room added to the Mansion to create a private office for himself. He used the study extensively, starting each day by shaving and dressing here at four or five o'clock in the morning. From here he wrote to political leaders across America and also managed Mount Vernon's 8,000 acres of farms, fisheries, mills and trades, meeting with his farm managers and overseers. Active as the study was, a relative once described it as "a place that none entered" without a direct order, giving Washington some relief from the bustling activity of Mount Vernon with its many visitors and large workforce. The simple, utilitarian decor of the study reflects George Washington's character. Many items are original, including the leather chair that he used throughout the eight years of his presidency

The Mount Vernon tour takes you on a journey through the grounds of the estate. You will see the rooms of the house as well as Washington's tomb and the Slave Memorial.

You can use the Site To Go utility to download the tour and have your students take the tour in pairs or teams. You might want to ask them specific questions for each part of their tour, just as you would if they were touring the museum in person. They can refer to the text as their museum docent and find the answers to the questions as they read the summaries on each page.

At this page of the tour, the Study, you might want to ask questions such as "For how many years was George Washington president?" and "Was Washington's study a public or private room and how do we know that?"

You could create a learning guide Web page for the students to follow as they read through the tour. As you create the Web page, think about mixing up the questions so they would have to re-visit a part of the tour several times as they follow through the questions. Provide links to the questions so students can just click on the link and find themselves at the appropriate part of the tour to find the answer.

MOUNT VERNON
EDUCATIONAL RESOURCES

Biographical   Grounds   George   Image Gallery   Online
Information   Tour   Washington   And Electronic   Quiz
                             and Slavery   Trading Cards

Text-Only Version

Please let us know how you are using this site.

○ Teacher ○ Student ○ Other

City: |_____| State: |___|

[Submit Query]

There are extensive educational resources for you to download and use. You can either choose parts of this resource packet to download or just use the Site To Go utility and schedule *Web Buddy* to download the entire site at a later time.

The sections of the resource packet are:

- Biographical Information
- Grounds Tour
- George Washington and Slavery
- Image Gallery and Electronic Trading Cards
- Online Quiz

The illustrated Biographical Information is written on a fifth grade level. It covers topics such as Washington's Colonial boyhood, his career and family, the Revolution, and his presidency.

The unit starts with an online true-false quiz which students can take before they read the lesson material and again afterward to see what they learned. This quiz works fine when you download it to your computer.

George Washington: True or False

HOW MUCH DO YOU KNOW ABOUT GEORGE WASHINGTON?

George Washington chopped down a cherry tree.	TRUE FALSE
George Washington had wooden teeth.	TRUE FALSE
George Washington once threw a silver dollar across the Potomac River.	TRUE FALSE
George Washington was the first president to live in the White House.	TRUE FALSE
George Washington wore a wig.	TRUE FALSE
George and Martha Washington had 2 children.	TRUE FALSE
George Washington was born on February 11, 1732.	TRUE FALSE
George Washington attended college.	TRUE FALSE
George Washington was the only founding father to free his slaves.	TRUE FALSE
George Washington was the first man to sign the U.S Constitution.	TRUE FALSE

The students click on the true or false buttons and are shown whether they answered correctly or incorrectly. If the answer is false, the Web page gives the information about the true side of the question.

George Washington - Commander in Chief

" .to see men without Cloathes to cover their nakedness, without Blankets to lay on, without Shoes, by which their Marches might be traced by the Blood from their feet... Marching through frost and Snow...and submitting to it all without a murmur, is a mark of patience and obedience, which in my opinion can scarce by parallel'd"

G.W. 1778 about the Continental Army

George Washington was chosen to lead the Continental Army during the Revolutionary War because of his reputation and experience. He had served as an officer in the French and Indian War and had completed several dangerous missions to the west. Washington was a daring leader, who used the element of surprise to win victory over British forces. Against great odds, he and his troops defeated the larger and better equipped British army, an astonishing feat that made Washington world-famous. His courage and determination helped inspire his troops and lead them to victory.

Military Stats
Continental Army in 1776...25,000
British Army in 1776...48,000

The Image Gallery contains famous photos of George Washington and summaries of the historical event that prompted the painting.

The Electronic Trading Cards are actually online greeting cards which can be sent via e-mail to another person if you are online. If you are using this Web site while offline, this option will not work. You might want to make sure you visit this page while you are online and send yourself each of the greeting cards so that you will receive the larger size graphics. You can then save them to disk or print them for use on a bulletin board or sign.

George Washington and Slavery

George Washington was born into a world in which slavery was accepted. He became a slave owner when his father died in 1743. At the age of eleven, he inherited ten slaves and 500 acres of land. When he began farming Mount Vernon eleven years later, at the age of 22, he had a work force of about 36 slaves. With his marriage to Martha Custis in 1759, 20 of her slaves came to Mount Vernon. After their marriage, Washington purchased even more slaves. The slave population also increased because the slaves were marrying and raising their own families. By 1799, when George Washington died, there were 316 slaves living on the estate.

The skilled and manual labor needed to run Mount Vernon was largely provided by slaves. Many of the working slaves were trained in crafts such as milling, coopering, blacksmithing, carpentry, and shoemaking. The others worked as house servants, boatmen, coachmen or field hands Some female slaves were also taught skills, particularly spinning, weaving and sewing, while others worked as house servants, in the laundry, the dairy, or the kitchen. Many female slaves also worked in the fields. Almost three-quarters of the 184 working slaves at Mount Vernon worked in the fields, and of these, about 60% were women.

The George Washington and Slavery section begins by telling students that he was born at a time when slavery was accepted. It continues to tell about the lives of the slaves at Mount Vernon. George Washington kept careful census records about the slaves and that gave much information to those historians studying slavery and Mount Vernon. This section gives a photo tour through the individual slave quarters and the family house. There are photographs showing what has been excavated during the archeological digs on the grounds.

There are two versions of the Online Quiz.

   1.   The Online Quiz requires you to actually be online. The answers are processed at the computer at Mount Vernon and students can work to improve their scores and times and then enter their names on the winners' list. You may want to edit the page to disable that option.

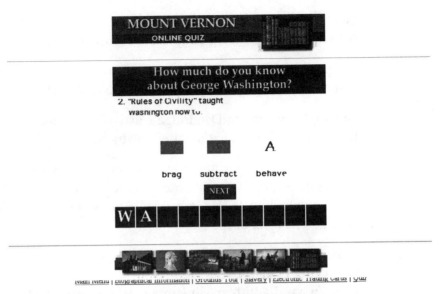

2. The Shockwave Quiz (shown above) requires that you have the Shockwave Plug-In for your Web browsing program (from Macromedia). It does work offline as long as you have the plug-in.

Students are given a question and buttons to click for the answers. As they correctly answer a question, a letter is filled in to finally spell WASHINGTON. There are even sound effects as they answer correctly or incorrectly.

By downloading the Educational Resources Web pages, you will have a terrific unit about George Washington and Mount Vernon ready for use on your computer. You may also want your students to do some additional research about George and Martha Washington. There are quite a few good sources of additional information online that you can download.

Other Washington Web Sites:

Colonial Williamsburg Foundation Homepage
(several Web pages about George Washington)
http://www.history.org/

George Washington in Williamsburg
http://www.history.org/people/bios/biowash1.htm

Biography of George Washington
http://www.history.org/people/bios/biowash2.htm

Biography of Martha Dandridge Custis Washington
http://www.history.org/people/bios/biomwash.htm

The above Web pages have extensive links to other pages. You should be careful if you choose to "download entire site." You may want to only download a Page To Go or use the Site To Go utility but only go one level deep.

General, President, Founding Father
(Benjamin Franklin Web site)
http://www.fi.edu/franklin/statsman/wshngtn.html

National Museum of American History—Timeline
http://www.si.edu/nmah/timeline/index.htm

Washington at War
http://www.si.edu/nmah/timeline/02wash.htm

White House—Biographies—George Washington
http://www.whitehouse.gov/WH/glimpse/presidents/html/gw1.html

HAIL TO THE CHIEF

There are a number of resources online about the Presidents of the United States. No, we don't mean the rock band—although there are a lot of sites online about them, too. Our presidents, from Washington and Lincoln to Reagan and Clinton, have assorted information about them scattered all over the Internet.

How are you going to bring all this information into your classroom so that your students can access it? How can you use this information as part of your lesson material?

White House

Let's start where the president lives. The White House maintains a Web site that brings a large quantity of information right to your fingertips.

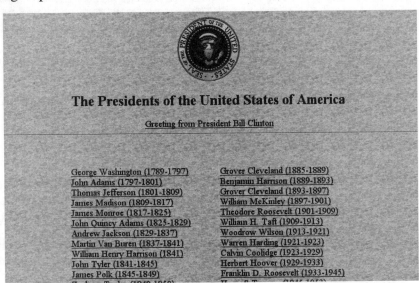

The Presidents of the United States of America

Greeting from President Bill Clinton

George Washington (1789-1797)
John Adams (1797-1801)
Thomas Jefferson (1801-1809)
James Madison (1809-1817)
James Monroe (1817-1825)
John Quincy Adams (1825-1829)
Andrew Jackson (1829-1837)
Martin Van Buren (1837-1841)
William Henry Harrison (1841)
John Tyler (1841-1845)
James Polk (1845-1849)

Grover Cleveland (1885-1889)
Benjamin Harrison (1889-1893)
Grover Cleveland (1893-1897)
William McKinley (1897-1901)
Theodore Roosevelt (1901-1909)
William H. Taft (1909-1913)
Woodrow Wilson (1913-1921)
Warren Harding (1921-1923)
Calvin Coolidge (1923-1929)
Herbert Hoover (1929-1933)
Franklin D. Roosevelt (1933-1945)

White House—The Presidents of the United States of America
http://www.whitehouse.gov/WH/glimpse/presidents/html/presidents.html

The Web pages contain portraits, links to speeches, and biographical information about each president. If you need information about the presidents, you can use the Site To Go utility to download these pages and use them on your computer as a teaching tool or reference tool for your students.

Franklin D. Roosevelt

Thirty-Second President 1933-1945

[Anna Eleanor Roosevelt]

Fast Fact: Franklin D. Roosevelt led the Nation through the Great Depression and World War II.

First Inaugural Address
Second Inaugural Address
Third Inaugural Address
Fourth Inaugural Address

Biography: Assuming the Presidency at the depth of the Great Depression, Franklin D. Roosevelt helped the American people regain faith in themselves. He brought hope as he promised prompt, vigorous action, and asserted in his Inaugural Address, "the only thing we have to fear is fear itself."

You can also find portraits and biographical information about the First Ladies at this URL.

http://www.whitehouse.gov/WH/glimpse/firstladies/html/firstladies.html

Also maintained by the White House, the pages contain information about the lives of the women behind the presidents.

But what about children? Didn't any children live in the White House? The White House for Kids Web site has been designed with children in mind. There is information there about the White House and the president, as well as photographs of the children who have lived in the White House, and even the pets who have lived there.

The White House for Kids
http://www.whitehouse.gov/WH/kids/html/home.html

Children in the White House

Many Presidents have had children or grandchildren who lived with them or visited often at the White House. Chelsea Victoria, daughter of Bill and Hillary Clinton, enjoys spending time with her father. Chelsea is the first child to live in the White House since Amy Carter. An avid soccer player and ballet enthusiast, Chelsea's favorite subjects in school are math and foreign languages.

Amy Carter, President Jimmy Carter's daughter, moved into the White House at the age of nine. She has three older brothers, named Jack, Jeff, and Chip. Amy's mother, Rosalynn, once remarked, "Her brothers are so much older that it is almost as though she has four fathers, and we have had to stand in line to spoil her."

President Richard Nixon's children, Tricia and Julie, along with Julie's husband, David Eisenhower, enjoyed family dinners in the White H...

Children in the White House
http://www.whitehouse.gov/WH/kids/html/children.html

Portraits of Presidents and First Ladies

By Popular Demand:
Portraits of the Presidents and First Ladies
1789-Present

Prints and Photographs Division, Library of Congress

Search by Keyword | **Browse** the Name and Subject Index

The Library of Congress has extensive resources for the study of the United States presidents and first ladies. Frequent requests for presidential portraits inspired Prints and Photographs Division staff to compile this ready reference aid of formal and informal pictures in the division's custody. The selected images include at least one likeness of each of the forty-one presidents and most of the first ladies. This presentation inaugurates a series of online illustrated reference aids that will appear under the running title "By Popular Demand"

Portraits of the Presidents and First Ladies
http://lcWeb2.loc.gov/ammem/odmdhtml/preshome.html

If you are looking for larger portraits of the presidents, the Library of Congress has them online at this Web site. "By Popular Demand" is a series of Web sites with information that has been in high demand from the Library.

The portrait graphics are in smaller thumbnail size as well as larger printable size. It would be a good idea to set this up using the Site To Go utility and schedule this download for during the night since it has such large graphics.

U. S. Presidents on Stamps

U.S. Presidents on Stamps

By David Cunningham

George Washington has appeared on more stamps than anyone else in history, but many people do not realize that every deceased President of the United States has had his place in the sun. Here we show the very first regular issue stamp showing George Washington, issued in 1847.

The Post Office Department (now known as the USPS) has issued two comprehensive sets of "Presidential" stamps. The first, back in 1938, and commonly called the "Prexies," consists of engravings of the Presidents from Washington to Coolidge, with the early Presidents all having a "Face Value" (Postage Value) the same as the order of their Presidency. In 1986, a series of sheetlets, each with nine stamps, was issued by the USPS, and ©USPS. These stamps show a "woodcut" of each President up to Lyndon Johnson. More recently, the USPS issued (©USPS) a Richard Nixon stamp.

Now you can look at many of these stamps by choosing them here. We may have a comment or two about the Presidents, but mainly we will let the images speak for themselves.

The Presidents of the United States

U.S. Presidents on Stamps
http://ourworld.compuserve.com/homepages/collect/stamps/uspres.html

Opening with a rousing midi rendition of "Hail to the Chief," this page houses an online exhibit of a collection of stamps with the portrait of presidents of the United States. If you're looking for an interesting way to illustrate your lessons about the presidents, this is it.

Mr. Cunningham, the collector, has been a stamp dealer for over 20 years. He has also included quotes from the presidents or comments about events that occurred during their terms.

Abraham Lincoln 1861 - 1865

"'A house divided against itself can not stand.' I believe this government cannot endure permanently half slave and half free."

"Nobody has ever expected me to be President. In my poor, lean, lank face nobody has ever seen that any cabbages were sprouting out."

Edward Everett made the main oration at the dedication of the cemetery at Gettysburg. Lincoln was to make only a few brief remarks. Yet those few remarks are now remembered.

More than one postage stamp has been included on most of the Web pages. Use the Site To Go utility to download this Web site and then let your students browse through the pages and pick out favorite stamps or make a list of the quotes. Have the students work in teams to find out who said what to solve the scavenger hunt.

United States Presidents Trivia

Another way to get the students actively searching through these Web sites you have downloaded is to give them trivia questions to solve. Eduzone has a list of trivia questions online and a corresponding answers list.

You could use the Site To Go utility to download the page and then use the list with your students. Don't let the students go to the answer page unless they are checking their work.

You could Convert the Web page into word processing pages and then print out the set of questions in order to allow the students to search for the answers without accessing that Web page. You could enlarge the font on that document and print a copy of the list to keep next to the computer. Students can find the answers when they have free time.

Presidential Trivia

The Eduzone wants to see how much you know about the Presidents.

1. who was the first President to be sworn into office by a woman?

2. which President ran for office unopposed?

3. Who was the first President to be visit a foreign country while in office?

4. Who was the oldest President upon leaving office?

5. Who were the only Presidents to be sworn into office by a former president?

6. who won the only Presidential election to be decided by Congress?

7. which President never got married?

8. Which former two Presidents died on the same day?

9. Name the Presidents who were assassinated.

10. Name the other Presidents who died in office?

11. Which President created the "Bull Moose Party"?

Presidential Trivia
http://www.eduzone.com/tips/PresidentTrivia/prestriv2htm.htm

History Buff's Home Page

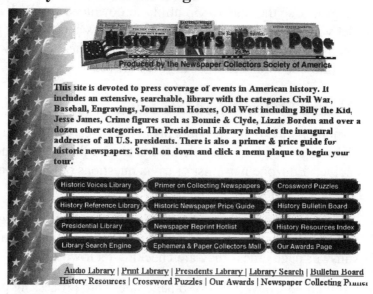

History Buff's Home Page
http://www.historybuff.com/

Rick Brown, the History Buff, has created an extensive Web site with information about the presidents and other historical events.

Facts About the United States Presidents			
George Washington -- First President			
Birthdate	**Birth Place**	**Occupations**	**Education**
February 12, 1732	Westmoreland Co. Virginia.	Surveyor, Tobacco Planter	Private
Parents Names	**Wife's Name**	**Marriage Year**	**Children**
Augustine Washington Mary Ball	Martha Dandridge Custis	1759	Step: Jacky, Patsy Adopted: Nelly, George
Political Party	**In Office**	**Vice President**	**Death Date**
None	1789-1797	John Adams	December 14, 1799
John Adams -- Second President			
Birthdate	**Birth Place**	**Occupations**	**Education**
October 30, 1735	Braintree/Quincy Mass.	Teacher, Lawyer	Harvard
Parents Names	**Wife's Name**	**Marriage Year**	**Children**
John Adams Susanna Boylston	Abigail Smith	1764	John Quincy, Thomas Charles, Abby
Political Party	**In Office**	**Vice President**	**Death Date**
Federalist	1797-1801	Thomas Jefferson	July 4. 1826

There is a table of data about each of the presidents. You could have students use this information to create a database and practice searching and sorting techniques.

Another large class project could be creating a time line of the presidents with this data posted on it as well as information from the Articles About Presidents or other Web sites you have downloaded. Include any pictures the students have printed.

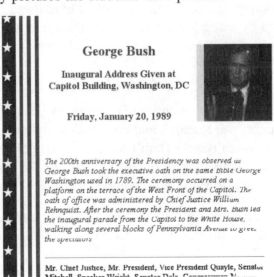

George Bush

Inaugural Address Given at Capitol Building, Washington, DC

Friday, January 20, 1989

The 200th anniversary of the Presidency was observed as George Bush took the executive oath on the same Bible George Washington used in 1789. The ceremony occurred on a platform on the terrace of the West Front of the Capitol. The oath of office was administered by Chief Justice William Rehnquist. After the ceremony the President and Mrs. Bush led the inaugural parade from the Capitol to the White House, walking along several blocks of Pennsylvania Avenue to greet the spectators

Mr. Chief Justice, Mr. President, Vice President Quayle, Senator Mitchell, Speaker Wright, Senator Dole, Congressman N...

Americana—United States Presidents

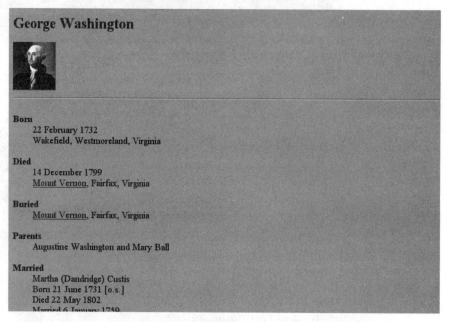

George Washington

Born
    22 February 1732
    Wakefield, Westmoreland, Virginia

Died
    14 December 1799
    Mount Vernon, Fairfax, Virginia

Buried
    Mount Vernon, Fairfax, Virginia

Parents
    Augustine Washington and Mary Ball

Married
    Martha (Dandridge) Custis
    Born 21 June 1731 [o.s.]
    Died 22 May 1802
    Married 6 January 1759

Americana—United States Presidents
http://www.lido.com/americana/presidents/

By using the Site To Go utility and downloading these presidential information pages, you could then use the files as templates for student projects. Students could add to these pages or you could edit them by leaving in the headings, leaving out all the data, and having teams of students fill in information about several presidents.

Presidents of the United States

This project is a wonderful example of what older elementary students can research and create. Kathy Prellwitz and Susie Mueller from South Beaver Dam Elementary School in Beaver Dam, WI, worked with a group of students as they did research about the presidents to fulfill a learning contract.

The learning contract information is also online and would be a wonderful project for you to start with your students. Let them compile information from the other sites you have downloaded. Then you can show them the final outcome of this group project.

 You could also convert one of the pages into a word processing document and then print it for your students to use as an example of the kind of information you would like them to find. The searching process, whether they are using books or Web pages, is the important concept in this project.

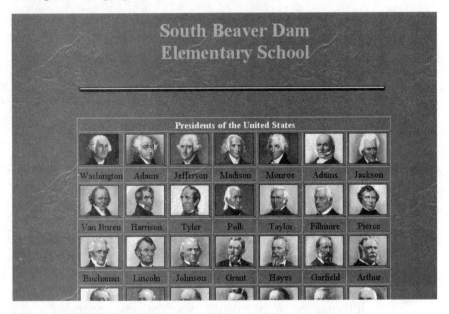

Presidents of the United States
http://www.peoples.net/~southbd/

These students found biographical information about each president, important events during his term, portraits of the presidents and first ladies, and American flags from that time period. They even found or scanned in graphics of a signature for each president.

This is a perfect time to use all the technology at your school. If you have a scanner, have the students scan images to include in their multimedia presentations or Web pages. If you have a digital camera, make this a special project by photographing the students while they are using other equipment and add those photographs to the final project.

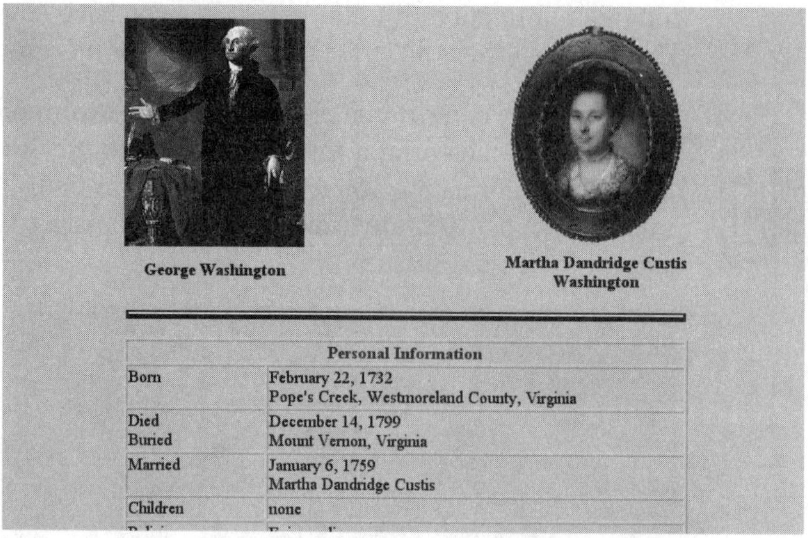

George Washington

Martha Dandridge Custis Washington

Personal Information	
Born	February 22, 1732 Pope's Creek, Westmoreland County, Virginia
Died Buried	December 14, 1799 Mount Vernon, Virginia
Married	January 6, 1759 Martha Dandridge Custis
Children	none

This shows part of a page from the student project. Your Web pages don't have to look this fancy, but make sure they are consistent in what they contain. Have graphics in the same place, and set up the information the same way on each page.

The data collected about each president includes personal information, interesting facts about his presidency, political information, and links to sources of information online. If you are doing this activity offline, let your students know the sources of information so they can let you know where they found certain data.

If you aren't able to have the students create Web pages or multimedia presentations, have them make posters of different presidents. Decide ahead of time whether you want the posters to follow a certain form or whether you want them to be individual creations.

You could also use a large sheet of roll paper—especially if you have a long hallway where you can hang this ongoing project. Make a time line of presidential terms and have the students decorate it with pictures they have printed from your collected Web pages or drawings they have done themselves. Have each student use the word processor to write a short report or an outline of information about his or her assigned president and post it on the time line.

They could add information about children in the White House during different presidential terms and can even include photos or pictures of the pets who lived there. They could continue to add to the time line as they found new information. This would be a terrific project during an election year—save space at the end for the new president!

Other President Web Sites:

Presidential Libraries IDEA Network
http://sunsite.unc.edu/lia/president/

Inaugural Addresses of the Presidents of the United States
1789–1989
http://www.columbia.edu/acis/bartleby/inaugural/index.html

American Memory from the Library of Congress
http://lcWeb2.loc.gov/

MSU Vincent Voice Library—President's Page
(sound recordings of speeches by presidents)
http://Web.msu.edu/vincent/presidents.html

Mount Rushmore
http://www.state.sd.us./tourism/rushmore/rushmore.html

Other Presidential Trivia Web Sites:

United States Presidents Trivia
http://synnergy.com/day/prestc.htm

Presidential Trivia
http://www.pbs.org/weta/citizens96/survival/trivia.html

Presidential Trivia
http://www.freep.com/news/inaug/trivia/index.htm

United States History Trivia
(a list of topics with trivia questions)
http://www.usahistory.com/trivia/

TOUR THE UNITED STATES

You live in one state and your students are learning about all the others. Where can you go to find current information quickly? These Web sites might just give you some answers.

Visit Your National Parks

What better way to see this vast country than to visit all of the National parks, seashores, historic sites, and monuments? You can take your students on a virtual trip of each state's treasures by visiting this Web site.

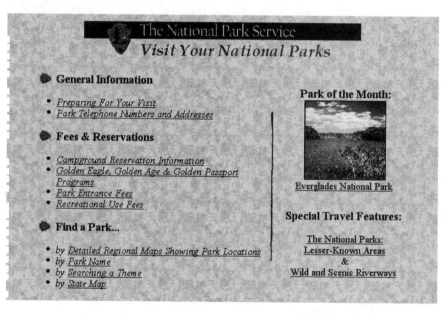

Visit Your National Parks
http://www.nps.gov/parks.html

By selecting the State Map, you will see a map of the United States which you can click on to access that state's Web page. Don't attempt to download this entire site. There is more information here than you and your students will need at any given time. You may just want to visit one state at a time.

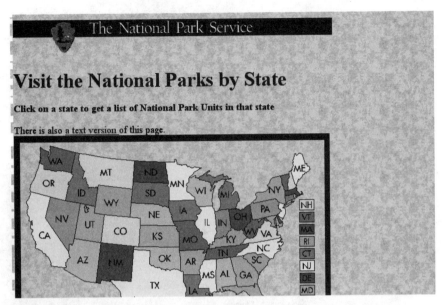

The state map page will look like this. If your browser doesn't handle graphics well, click on the hypertext link to go to the text only pages. If this map loads all right, you can simply click on the state of your choice.

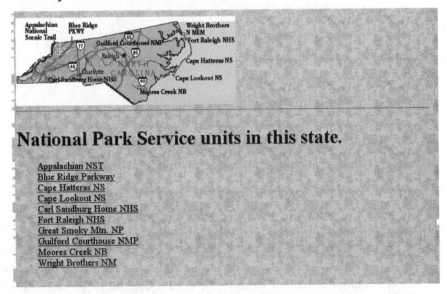

National Park Service units in this state.

Appalachian NST
Blue Ridge Parkway
Cape Hatteras NS
Cape Lookout NS
Carl Sandburg Home NHS
Fort Raleigh NHS
Great Smoky Mtn. NP
Guilford Courthouse NMP
Moores Creek NB
Wright Brothers NM

Each state page includes a map showing the location of the parks and is a hypertext link index of all the parks in that state.

You might want to use the Site To Go utility from the state page and set it to take that page and go one level deep in order to get the state and all its National Parks.

The Web page for each park has a brief description of the history of that site and when it was established as a National Park, Seashore, or Site. In addition to photographs of the area, the page also has information such as:

- suggested time of year to visit
- climate
- directions to the park
- transportation available
- NPS facilities
- recommended park activities
- special events
- nearby attractions
- address to write for more information

Students could create a database and fill in specific data as you study each state's parks. You could also use this with a science class studying oceans or mountains and use the Page To Go utility to download several representative seashore Web pages or mountain park Web pages.

Students could also use this and other data in a language arts class to create a travel brochure for a state. They could incorporate information found at the Web site and original artwork or graphics into a word processing document and print the brochure. If you don't have that technology available, they could print the pictures they want and write the brochure by hand.

 You might want to take your students on a virtual vacation each month. You can start with the National Park Service's Web site and use their "Park of the Month." Download the information about that park and then find additional Web sites about that area. Create a Web page index and have the students visit all your downloaded sites as they tour your monthly vacation spot.

PostcardsFrom.com

PostcardsFrom.com
http://www.postcardsfrom.com/index.html

For those of us who always say, "One of these years, I'm going to quit my job and travel around the country," here is a Web site that proves that it can be done. Priscilla Sarsfield, writer and researcher, and her husband, Ken Mahlenkamp, photographer and designer, have done just that.

They are traveling throughout the 50 states and have created a Web site so that you can follow along on their travels. Even if they are finished with their trip by the time you get this book, their Web site will stay up and they may even be adding teacher resources to it.

Once they decided to go on their journey, they realized that they would need to send postcards home to all their family and friends. They would probably pick up more friends along the way who would be interested in how the rest of the trip was going, too, so they decided to create an online postcard each day to share their journey.

They visit important landmarks and sites in each state and return to their motor home each night where Ken uses the digital photographs he has taken that day to create an original "digital postcard" to share with the world.

The Web site also contains pages with fun facts about each state they visit and a map graphic to show the state. This would be a great way to visit most of the states with your students in a school year. You could share this information with them each week even after Priscilla and Ken's journey is over.

They have even designed an information page for each state visited which includes a special "stamp" for the State Flower, Bird, Tree, Flag, and other special state emblems. Students could type that information into a database each week and compare states that share common emblems. There are several states which share the same State Bird, for example. Once they get data on a number of states, they'll start to see those similarities.

By using information from Web sites like these, students could work in teams and create state advertising posters. This would be a good project for practicing persuasive writing skills and developing organization and design skills. They could use the Web pages as guides for their own artwork and text.

Other U. S. Travel Web Sites:

Cyberwonders: Travel North America
http://www.cyberwonders.com/travelusa.html

The Fifty States of the United States
(state capitals, birds, and songs)
http://www.scvol.com/States/fileindx.htm

LIGHTHOUSES: FUNCTION OR FANCY

In order to utilize resources found online, this activity uses a simple Web page that you can create or edit with hyperlinks to downloaded Web sites which are now saved on your computer.

This could be a center activity or one of many individual mini-lessons you could have stored on your computer for the students to choose to do when they have completed other regular classroom work.

The basic page is meant to be a starting point for the students. It is a means by which you can organize Web sites you downloaded by using *Web Buddy*'s Site To Go process. It is also where you will pose the questions you want your students to answer.

Lighthouses: Function or Fancy?
http://www.geocities.com/Athens/1573/activities/lighthouses.html

You can use the Page To Go utility to download this page and use it as a template guide for adding your own questions or listing the resources you have downloaded to your computer. Choose resources which will have answers to your questions.

You can use the Edit function on your browser to edit this page once you have downloaded it. The HTML lines with "http://" references to Web sites online should be changed to show where your downloaded Web sites reside on your computer.

The questions are simple text and can be freely edited to suit the concept you are studying and the age level of the students.

Add graphics to increase student interest whenever you are creating your own Web page activity. In this case, digital photographs and a scanned photo have been added to the Web page to let the students know what the subject of the activity is.

In The Park—Online Newsletter

A good source for lighthouse information would be the National Park Service in areas such as Cape Hatteras, North Carolina, where there are lighthouses at National Seashore locations.

In The Park—Online Newsletter of The National Park Service
http://www.nps.gov/caha/itp.htm

Florida Lighthouse Page

The Florida Lighthouse Page has information such as location, history, keepers, current data, and tour information about each of the lighthouses found in Florida.

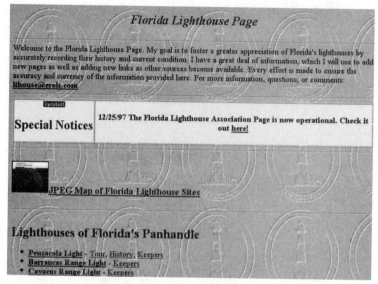

Florida Lighthouse Page
http://www.erols.com/lthouse/home.htm

If you are working with younger children, keep the number of lighthouse pages to a minimum and ask questions such as:

- What does a lighthouse do?
- How old are lighthouses?

This would be a good time to use a KWL chart and have your students tell you what they Know about lighthouses, what they Want to know about them, and then fill in things they have Learned about lighthouses.

With older students, you can pose questions such as:

- Are lighthouses still in operation?
- When were most lighthouses built? Why might that be so?
- Have any lighthouses ever been successfully moved?
- Are any lighthouses in danger of being washed into the ocean?
- Were lighthouses only built in North America?

Other Lighthouse Web Sites:

Lighthouses of Martha's Vineyard
http://mvy.com/lighthouses.html

The Homepage of Lighthouses
http://www.worldlights.com/world/

Lighthouses Along the Delaware-Maryland Coast
http://www.beach-net.com/lighthouses.html

Lighthouses
http://www.creative-visions.com/lighthse.htm

Links: Lighthouses and Lightships
http://pc-78-120.udac.se:8001/WWW/Nautica/Pointers/Lighthouses.html

Lighthouse Links on the Internet
http://www.lhbs.com/lhlinks.htm

LEARNING YOUR WAY AROUND MAPS

There are as many reasons for teaching map skills to students of all ages as there are types of maps. But have you ever tried to talk about a specific location or a type of map and not been able to find one to illustrate your point? We're going to look at several map sites which you can use to download maps or teaching materials to help you and your students.

Houghton Mifflin Co.—Social Studies Center

If you've been looking for a map to print as part of a student worksheet or activity, then you should visit this Web site.

Social Studies Center
Copyright c 1998 Houghton Mifflin Company. All Rights Reserved.
http://www.eduplace.com/ss/index.html

They have Social Studies lesson plans online and links to current events for you to visit for additional teaching materials. There is also a long list of printable and reproducible maps available for you to download. You could schedule *Web Buddy*'s Site To Go utility and download all of them one evening to have them available on your computer whenever you need them.

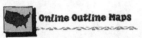

Below is a selection of outline maps for use in the classroom or at home. Feel free to print or download any of these maps for your personal use in activities, reports, or stories.

- Africa: Political
- Africa: Political and Physical
- Asia and the South Pacific: Political
- Central America: Political
- Colonial America, 1776
- Eastern Hemisphere
- Europe: Political
- European Countries
- North America
- North America: Political

Houghton Mifflin Co. Online Outline Maps
Copyright c 1998 Houghton Mifflin Company. All Rights Reserved.
http://www.eduplace.com/ss/ssmaps/index.html

If you are using a word processing program to create student worksheets, you could import a map graphic into the document and use it as the basis for a map skills activity. (Physically "cutting and pasting" is a thing of the past.)

You could use the graphics files in a graphics editing program and color various parts or add labels where you want them. You could have the students use the World map or U.S. map and color the country or state they are researching. Then they could print their graphic and use it in a report or on a poster.

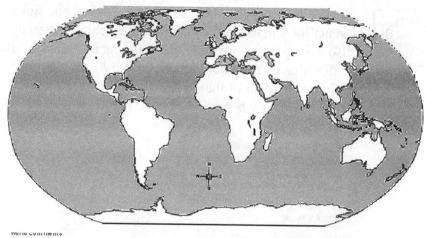

World Continents
Copyright (c) 1996 Houghton Mifflin Company. All rights reserved

Copyright © 1998 Houghton Mifflin Company. All Rights Reserved.

Even primary grade students could open a graphics file such as the world map and color the continents and print it in color. You might want to save a black and white graphic for each student under his or her name so that he or she can open his or her own file to color each day.

You could also have a disk for each student if he or she goes to a computer lab and have the same file name on each disk. Then you could instruct the students to open "mapfile" on their disks and color a particular continent.

Graphic Maps

If you and your students are going to be creating multimedia projects or Web pages about countries around the world or states in the U. S., you might want to download some graphics or map images that are already in color.

The Graphic Maps site has quite a few graphics showing states and countries and their location in relation to the rest of the continent. They are available for you to download using the Site To Go utility and then you can make them available to your students.

A Graphic Maps collection of original cartography including cities, continents, countries, exotic travel destinations, globes, flags and world atlas images.

Geography DAILY PRIZES Click Here! QUIZ

Link Exchange Member

http://www.graphicmaps.com
Developing cartographic images and custom maps for applications worldwide from
LATITUDE - 29° 14' 45" North - LONGITUDE - 94° 31' 16" West

CARTOGRAPHIC IMAGES

From the selections below, download and use
the image(s) of your choice at no-charge!

WORLD IMAGES
U.S. IMAGES
GLOBES
FLAGS
COUNTRIES
CONTINENTS
COMPASSES

Graphic Maps
http://www.graphicmaps.com/

Pensacola Lighthouse

- Location Map
- History
- List of Keepers
- The Lighthouse Today
- Getting there
- Tour the lighthouse

Go back to Main Menu.

Created: 1/31/96
Last Updated: 03/01/96
Web Authors: Neil Hurley
For more information, questions, or comments: lihouse@gmail.com
Copyright 1996 Historic Lighthouse Publishers

There are images of the world, the states, and various countries. You
might want to schedule *Web Buddy* to download the site at night
since there is a large quantity of graphics file.

There is also a list of atlas graphics that you could download to have a graphic with more detail about certain locations.

NORTH AMERICA

Antigua is a major tourist destination with numerous resorts and great beaches. It's a popular port-of-call for cruise ships and jumbo jets from around the world. The capital city is **St John's,** the currency is the *East Caribbean Dollar,* the official language is *English* and it's home to 67,000 people. **Barbuda** is approximately 30 miles to the north. It offers terrific fishing, snorkeling and a collection of shipwrecks to explore.

GO TO

ANTIGUA/BARBUDA
Facts/Figures/Flag
Internet Links

Caribbean Maps
North America Page
WorldAtlas.Com

These graphics could also be used by you in worksheets and special activities if you import them into a word processing document. Having them readily available is also important if there is a current event in a location and you need a map to include with lesson materials.

You could also print these from a color deskjet or inkjet printer onto special overhead transparency film and use them as teaching tools with your projector. Remember when printing overhead transparencies you need to use the correct film (for printers) and you need to increase the amount of ink you use in your printer.

You need to make this choice in your printer setup when you instruct the computer to print the page. There should be a setting for paper type—change it to "transparency" and then print. This will apply more ink to the transparency and make the colors more vivid. It will also take longer for the transparency to dry, so print it and then set it aside for a while.

What Do Maps Show?

Now that you have all these maps at your disposal, do your students know how to read them? The U.S. Geological Survey has several lesson plans (with all the materials you need to teach them) online at their Web site.

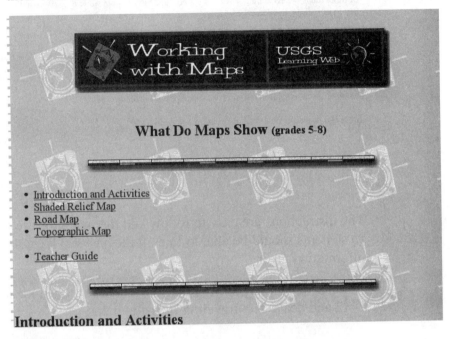

What Do Maps Show (grades 5-8)

- Introduction and Activities
- Shaded Relief Map
- Road Map
- Topographic Map

- Teacher Guide

Introduction and Activities

USGS: What Do Maps Show 5–8
http://info.er.usgs.gov/education/teacher/what-do-maps-show/index.html

"What Do Maps Show" is a lesson plan for students in grades 5–8. It teaches geographic themes such as location, place, relationship, movement, and regions. Students will learn about different types of maps—shaded relief, road, and topographic.

You can use the Site To Go utility to download the lesson plans, teacher guide, worksheets, and student instruction pages. You can then print them out and have each student fill out the worksheets, or have the students work in pairs or teams to access the instructions on your computer and answer the questions on plain paper.

What Do Maps Show: Activity Sheet #3
What You Can Learn From a Map

There are different maps for different purposes. In this lesson, you'll learn more about the special uses of three maps -- a road map, a shaded relief map, and a topographic map. Remember, the legend is the key to unlocking the secrets of a map.

Road Maps

Road maps show people how they can travel from one place to another. They also show some physical features, such as mountains and rivers, and politicial features, such as cities and towns.

Find and draw the map symbol for an interstate highway.

Find and draw the map symbol for a State highway.

The instructions are easy to follow and the materials are all included so students should be able to find all the answers from the information given.

Another lesson, Exploring Maps, is geared toward students in grades 7–12 and deals with traveling by using maps.

Map Adventures

The USGS has also created a map lesson unit for younger children in grades K–3. They will learn basic concepts for seeing things from different perspectives and learning how to use simple maps.

The lessons in this unit are:

> View From the Ground
> View from a Higher Point
> View from Overhead
> Symbols and Legends
> Learning Directions on a Map
> Map Grids
> Map Scale

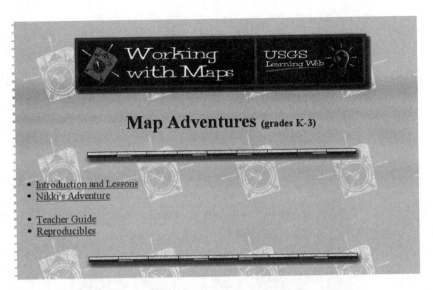

USGS: Map Adventures K–3
http://www.usgs.gov/education/learnWeb/MA/index.html

The lessons in the unit are based on the story of a little girl who visits an imaginary amusement park. She goes up in a hot air balloon and gets a different view of the amusement park. (The story is available for you to download.)

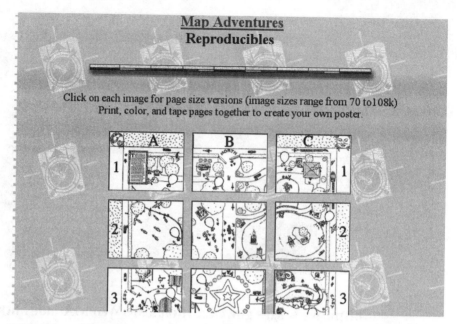

There is also a series of 15 full page graphics which you can print and then tape together to create a LARGE map of the amusement park. You should schedule *Web Buddy* to download this site at a time when you are not busy at the computer. These are large graphics and will take a while to download. Once you have them on your computer, you will be able to access and print them quickly without having to spend time online.

Other Map Web Sites:

The Great Globe Gallery
(graphics of globes)
http://hum.amu.edu.pl/~zbzw/glob/glob1.htm

International Maps From Around the World
(index to other map sites)
http://www.tradezone.com/maps.htm

The Maps Links
(out of the frame—so you can bookmark the other sites)
http://www.tradezone.com/mapslnks.htm

US Geological Survey—Flagstaff Field Center Index
http://wwwflag.wr.usgs.gov/USGSFlag/menu/FFCindex.html

USGS Flagstaff—Digital Elevation Model Shaded Relief Maps
(Western U. S. state images)
http://wwwflag.wr.usgs.gov/USGSFlag/Data/shadedRel.html

Teaching in the Learning Web at the USGS
(other geological lesson units available)
http://www.usgs.gov/education/learnWeb/index.html

Helping Your Child Learn Geography
(a teaching packet for parents and children)
http://www.ed.gov/pubs/parents/Geography/index.html

WEBQUEST—HOW WE GET AROUND

Now that you have found so many wonderful resources online, how do you guide your students to visit those Web pages with a purpose?

Bernie Dodge, a professor of educational technology at San Diego State University, devised a lesson plan format that has become a standard for teacher-developed "Web lessons." This approach can be used to teach any subject area to students of any grade level.

There are templates posted online at:

Student Lesson Template
http://edWeb.sdsu.edu/Webquest/LessonTemplate.html

Teacher's Guide Template
http://edWeb.sdsu.edu/Webquest/TeacherLessonTemplate.html

You can save those templates to disk and edit them within your browser's editing utility or a simple editing program. Then use the "Save As" function to save them with new names and have your students use the Student Lesson to guide them through the activities.

The format for a lesson follows these simple steps:

- Introduction
- Task
- Resources
- Process
- Evaluation
- Conclusion

You can provide links in the Resources section that connect to sites online (if you are online at your classroom computer) or to Web pages you have downloaded.

How We Get Around

The following is a sample of a WebQuest written to help students learn about the history of the different types of transportation.

Introduction | Task | Resources | Process | Evaluation | Conclusion

Introduction

Early man simply walked around to get from place to place. Then he realized that there might be more food or a better cave farther away. Once he got tired of walking, man started thinking of better and easier ways to travel. As you answer these questions, think about why each form of travel or transportation was invented.

The Task

As you answer the following questions, keep notes or draw pictures of the different forms of transportation. You will then use this information to create a timeline of the development of travel.

- How were wheels first used?
- What were some of the uses for the first large boats?
- Who invented the first automobile?
- What was invented to allow more than a few passengers to travel in a vehicle with wheels?
- Where could trains travel?
- When did man first fly?
- Who had the first successful flights of an airplane?
- When was the first manned flight to outer space?
- When did the Space Shuttle first fly?

How We Get Around
http://www.geocities.com/Athens/1573/activities/transquest.html

This is the student lesson page. The Introduction simply lets the students know what this lesson is about. It might include a problem that they need to solve or a scenario in which they might find themselves.

The task lets them know what will be accomplished and lists any questions they need to address while they are searching through the Web sites.

The Teacher's Guide Web page would give clues to other teachers as to what the expected learning goal is and why these tasks were chosen to accomplish that goal. The Teacher's Guide Web page to accompany this lesson can be found by clicking on the link at the upper left-hand corner of the student page or at this URL:

http://www.geocities.com/Athens/1573/activities/transteach.html

The Teacher's Guide is divided into similar sections with a few additions:

Introduction
Content Areas—subject areas studied
Standards—which standards of learning correlate
Implementation—how will this be taught, how many days, etc.
Resources—what will students need to complete the task
Entry Skills—what should they know in advance
Evaluation—how will you evaluate their learning
Variations—how you can change this for different learning abilities
Conclusion

Resources

You can use these websites to find the answers to your questions. Remember to keep track of any other forms of transportation that you find during your search for answers. These may be included in your timeline, as well.

The Burgwardt Bicycle Museum has information about the history of pedaling.

At the Henry Ford Museum & Greenfield Village Online, you can visit exhibits about early automobiles.

The Walker Transportation Collection includes historic planes, automobiles, fire engines, buses, trains, and boats.

Take a train-ride on the Union Pacific Railroad and learn some facts about the history of trains.

Visit the Komoka Railway Museum to learn more about railroad history.

If you want to learn about hot air balloons, visit Mark Powell's Hot Air Balloon website.

At Those Magnificent Men and Their Flying Machines, you will learn about the first airplanes.

The Illustrated History of Boeing Aircraft shows everything they've created, from biplanes to helicopters to the Space Shuttle.

At the National Air & Space Museum in Washington, DC, you can tour the history of flight from the Wright Brothers to flights to the moon and the current Space Shuttle program.

The Resources section lets the students know what materials they can use to find the answers. In this case, the Web sites are listed with a little information as to what they will find at each one. You could put these in order with your task questions or mix them up. With younger children, you might want to mix the Task and Resources sections so that each question is immediately followed by the corresponding Web page.

This WebQuest has the students researching through Web sites about different forms of transportation. One purpose of this is to find data for the time line.

The other purpose would be for them to find illustrations to put on that time line.

The Process

Your team should visit one or two of the websites each day and try to find the answers to the questions. While you are at the website, find any other information about transportation that you would like to include in your timeline. The more information you find, the more complete you can make your timeline.

1. Find the answer to each question.
2. Find pictures to illustrate your timeline.
3. Browse for any additional information to include.
4. Think about why each of these inventions was created. What was the original need? What are they used for, now? Add this kind of information to your timeline data.
5. Once you think you have a complete set of information, you may get roll paper and create your timeline of transportation.

Make sure you keep accurate notes of the types of transportation and the years when it was first being developed. Keep records of where you found the information, in case you need to go back to clarify something.

Organize all of your data BEFORE starting to create your timeline. Make a rough draft on regular paper to make sure you haven't left out any steps in the development of transportation.

The Process lets them know what they should be finding in their activities and what they will have to do with the information once they find it. It gives them some guidelines to let them know about the expected outcome.

Evaluation

You will be graded according to how complete your timeline is. You should have information on it that shows that you found the answers to the questions above. Your grade will improve if you put additional information on the timeline. Your timeline must also be in correct chronological order

Conclusion

Through your searching, you should find that there were always reasons for the developments of new forms of transportation. Newer forms of transportation sometimes relied on parts of the methods that already existed. Think about that as you create your timeline - what old "technology" did each new invention use?

The Evaluation tells them how their learning will be evaluated or graded. It tells them your expectations about the final product. You can be more or less specific as needed.

The Conclusion lets them know what they should have learned while they were doing this activity. This acts as a guideline throughout the lesson.

Union Pacific Railroad

Facts and Figures

- Company Overview of the Union Pacific Railroad
- Maps of Union Pacific
- U.S. Guide to the Union Pacific Railroad --state-by-state railroad operations and related maps
- Superlatives: Tracks
- Superlatives: Bridges
- Bailey Yard
- Roster of UPRR Locomotive Ownership
- AC Locomotives
- Locomotive Horn Signal.

History and Photos

- Union Pacific Railroad History --historical information on the railroad and its evolution
- Photo Gallery --numerous images from the extensive Union Pacific Museum photo collection

Union Pacific Railroad—Facts, Figures, and History
http://www.uprr.com/uprr/ffh/

This is one of the sites your students would visit as part of that WebQuest.

You could download this section of the Web site using the Site To Go utility and your students could access it on your computer in order to answer the questions posed. There is an extensive section at the Union Pacific Railroad Web site devoted to Fact, Figures, and History in an attempt to educate the public about the history of trains and the railroad system.

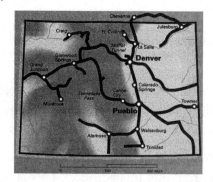

There is a railway system for every state the Union Pacific Railroad travels through.

You could use these maps as part of a lesson about traveling in the western part of the United States by having students describe their train trip through several states you are studying.

Classes of Locomotive:

Big Boy: The world's largest steam locomotive, twenty-five Big Boys were built exclusively for Union Pacific, the first of which was delivered in 1941. The locomotives were 132 feet long and weighed 1.2 million pounds. Because of their great length, the frames of the Big Boys were "hinged," or articulated, to allow them to negotiate curves. They had a 4-8-8-4 wheel arrangement, which meant they had four wheels on the leading set of "pilot" wheels which guided the engine, eight drivers, another set of eight drivers, and four wheels following which supported the rear of the locomotive. The massive engines normally operated between Ogden, Utah and Cheyenne, Wyoming.

Although there are no Big Boys left in operation today, eight of them were eventually donated for public display in various cities around the country. They can be found in Los Angeles, California; St. Louis, Missouri; Dallas, Texas; Omaha, Nebraska; Denver, Colorado; Scranton, Pennsylvania; Green Bay, Wisconsin; and Cheyenne, Wyoming.

Challenger: Union Pacific at one time owned 105 Challenger locomotives. Built between 1936 and 1943, the Challengers were nearly 122 feet long and weighed over one million pounds. Articulated like their big brother, the Big Boy, the Challengers had a 4-6-6-4 wheel arrangement. They operated over most of the Union Pacific system, primarily in freight service, but a few were assigned to passenger trains operating through mountain territory to California and Oregon.

Students will be able to find photographs of early steam locomotives and currently used trains.

Komoka Railway Museum

This is another site for your students to visit on their quest for information about the railroad system and trains.

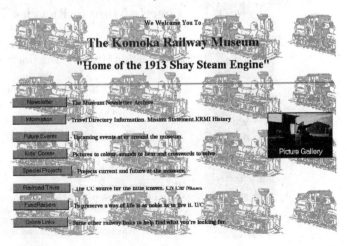

Komoka Railway Museum
http://www.komokarail.ca/

Special Projects at the Museum

The Baggage Car

As you can see, the Pre-1939 Canadian National baggage car is more than ready for a facelift while doubling as a "jigger shed", the unit is undergoing the repairs necessary to once again accept "passengers". The roof has been patched and primed to keep the elements out. The exterior skin has recently been sandblasted and epoxy primed by a local contractor. As soon as some welding and patching has been completed, the finish painting will take place. When completed, plans are to have the baggage car house a theatre and the museums model railroad

 This shows one of the projects at the museum, and is just one of the many photographs of historic railroad equipment that your students will find. You may want to use the Site To Go utility to download all the information there or you may just want to download representative photographs of trains and handcars to use with a bulletin board display or poster.

Burgwardt Bicycle Museum

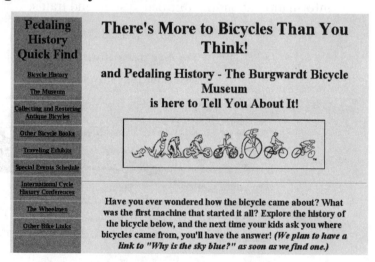

Pedaling History Quick Find

Bicycle History

The Museum

Collecting and Restoring Antique Bicycles

Other Bicycle Books

Traveling Exhibits

Special Events Schedule

International Cycle History Conferences

The Wheelmen

Other Bike Links

There's More to Bicycles Than You Think!

and Pedaling History - The Burgwardt Bicycle Museum is here to Tell You About It!

Have you ever wondered how the bicycle came about? What was the first machine that started it all? Explore the history of the bicycle below, and the next time your kids ask you where bicycles came from, you'll have the answer! *(We plan to have a link to "Why is the sky blue?" as soon as we find one.)*

Burgwardt Bicycle Museum
http://members.aol.com/bicyclemus/bike_museum/PedHist.htm

Your students will find information about the history of bicycles and all the many types at this museum's Web site. You can use the Site To Go utility to download the history of bicycles and let them take a virtual tour all the way back to the days of bikes without wheels.

The Velocipede or Boneshaker

The next appearance of a two-wheeled riding machine was in 1865, when pedals were applied directly to the front wheel. This machine was known as the velocipede ("fast foot"), but was popularly known as the bone shaker, since it was also made entirely of wood, then later with metal tires, and the combination of these with the cobblestone roads of the day made for an extremely uncomfortable ride. They also became a fad, and indoor riding academies, similar to roller rinks, could be found in large cities.

The High-Wheel Bicycle

 Pictures of early bicycles are described with historical information. You could also Convert this Web page and then print as overhead transparencies to show the entire class. (Remember to use inkjet or deskjet transparency film and to set your printer to print transparency quality so that there is more ink on the film.)

The Walker Transportation Collection

This is an online museum exhibit of photographs of different types of transportation used in the New England area.

There are photos and information about:

airplanes	railroads
automobiles	ships & boats
buses	trolleys
fire engines	trucks

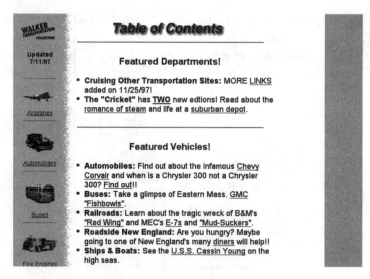

Walker Transportation Museum
http://www.tiac.net/users/fletcher/index.html

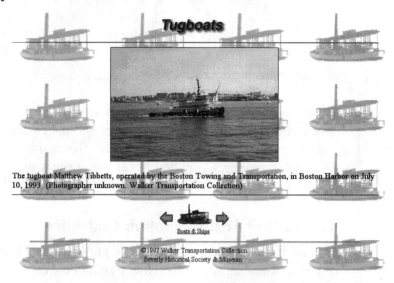

The tugboat Matthew Tibbetts, operated by the Boston Towing and Transportation, in Boston Harbor on July 10, 1993. (Photographer unknown. Walker Transportation Collection)

© 1997 Walker Transportation Collection
Beverly Historical Society & Museum

The photographs could be used by your students on their time lines. Some students might want to create multimedia presentations as their time line projects. Once the projects are completed, you and your students might want to take photographs and let these online museum Webmasters know how you used their information. There are e-mail addresses at all the Web sites.

Other Transportation Web Sites:

Igor I. Sikorsky Historical Archives, Inc.
http://www.iconn.net/igor/index.html

Henry Ford Museum & Greenfield Village Online
http://www.hfmgv.org/

Mark Powell's Hot Air Balloon
http://Web2.airmail.net/markpowl/balloon.html

Those Magnificent Men and Their Flying Machines
http://www.ozemail.com.au/~flying/index.html

Illustrated History of Boeing Aircraft
http://www.boeing.com/companyoffices/history/

National Air & Space Museum
http://www.nasm.edu/

Other WebQuest Web Sites:

The WebQuest Page
http://edWeb.sdsu.edu/Webquest/Webquest.html

Web Quest
http://www.lfelem.lfc.edu/tech/DuBose/Webquest/wq.html

Lesson Plan WebQuest
http://www.shastalink.k12.ca.us/telementors/quest.html

WebQuests
University of New Mexico
http://www.unm.edu/~jeffryes/PEN.html

Regional Education Technology Assistance (RETA) Initiative
Examples of WebQuests
http://www.unm.edu/~jeffryes/RETA/examplewq.html

ON WALKABOUT DOWN UNDER

Take your class on a trip to Australia—a virtual trip, that is! With access to the Internet, Australia is at your fingertips—not halfway around the world. You can download information from a variety of Web sites and let your students explore the cities and outback as they learn about the land "down under."

To find out what is happening in Australia as you are studying the country, use *Web Buddy* to download some of the daily online newspapers. Use a newspaper index like Internet Press to locate the newspapers.

Internet Press

Internet Press
http://www.club.innet.be/~year0230/link4.htm

This site has newspaper links from around the world. Many radio stations and television networks have online publications and those are listed here, also. Just find the country you are studying and visit the newspapers.

The Sydney Morning Herald

The Sydney Morning Herald
http://www.smh.com.au/

Have your students read through the newspapers and compare life in Australia with life in their cities and towns. They should notice that Australia's seasons are the opposite of those in the United States.

They will be able to read about different holidays and customs as they are being celebrated.

Post Newspapers Online

Students will enjoy exploring a different country through its news articles and local stories. Use the Site To Go utility to download this newspaper and retrieve all the articles.

Post Newspapers Online
http://www.postnewspapers.com.au/

This homeless galah is winning the hearts of staff
at the Subiaco Veterinary Hospital

Where else will you read a quote like, "Staff at the Subiaco Veterinary Hospital have fallen in love with a bird that went walkabout"? Have your students read through the articles to find Aussie slang and then have them find the definitions in one of several online "Slang Dictionaries."

OzENews

OzENews

Australian News direct to your InBox

Headlines
Economic boost for Howard - The Australian
PM attacks Hanson's `ugly' claim - The Age
Indonesia asks Downer to throw trade lifeline - Sydney Morning Herald
Airlines slash European fares as Asia bites - Financial Review
Govt ministers to inspect flood situation - ABC
Talented find pretty penny in graffiti gone legal - The Australian
MFP failure leaves a red-faced nation - The Australian
Clinton: 'I Did Not Have Sexual Relations With That Woman, Miss Lewinsky' - CNN

Business
Rio pockets $21m from Hunter cuts - The Australian
Competition is fierce for the business of education - The Age
Gains have made property trusts groovy - Sydney Morning Herald
Sell-offs to win States $80bn by 2000 - Financial Review
International Markets Update - South China Morning Post

Information
IBM Australia wins $10m Qantas deal - Financial Review
Digital rivals in NFF showdown - Financial Review
Revenue dangers for groupware - Financial Review
Telstra offloads IPND - ComputerWorld Today
Internet News and Views - The Inside Running is an independent, free email newsletter reporting and commenting on Internet News

27 January 1998

Have OzENews emailed to you every morning. Just Click the Button once.

Subscribe

Miss a few days this Week? Click here for OzENews Weekly.

OzENews
http://www.ozemail.com.au/~gillespi/index.html

This Web page has links to headline news in other newspapers and sends a daily or weekly news e-mail if you sign up for it. This would be a good site to schedule to download and check for interesting news to share with your students each morning while you are studying Australia.

Australian A to Z Animal Archive

If you want to learn more than just what the people of Australia are doing, you might want to look at this archive of information about the animals of the continent.

From Antechinus to Zyzomys, this site has information about every animal in Australia. If they're missing one, ask them and they'll find information for you. This would be a terrific resource to download using the Site To Go utility and keep on your computer for reference.

Australian A - Z Animal Archive

* This site is a community service of the AAA World Announce Archive - Matilda Search Engine in Sydney, Australia.
  A link to us on your site would be appreciated.

Australian Animal Archive

Welcome to our Archive of Animals from the Great Southern Island Continent Australia. We've arranged a listing of most native creatures whose name co-incides with the letters of the alphabet. This Australian Animal Archive is constantly being updated.
If you would like to know about an animal that we haven't yet included in this directory please let us know. To enter the archive simply click on the arrow head icon at the end of the below link.

Australian A to Z Animal Archive
http://www.aaa.com.au/A_Z/

Echidna

An Echidna is a mammal and resembles the Porcupine. It is also called the Spiny Anteater. An Echidna's body is covered with long sharp spines set in short fur. These spines are the Echidnas defence mechanism. When attacked it rolls itself in a tight ball and burrows out of reach.

Echidnas have no teeth, but uses a long sticky tongue to penetrate ant and termite nests, which they have ripped open with their strong ripping claws

The Echidna has no fixed abode except when the female is suckling its young. Shelter is where ever the echidna finds it and this could be in logs, under bushes or in caves. They are 35 - 45 cms long and can weigh 2-7 kg. Just like the Platypus, the Echidna has a spur on its ankle but it is not poisonous like the Platypus

Emu

The Emu is the second largest bird in the world (The Ostrich is the biggest). It is Australia's largest bird standing 1.5 metres high and weighing up to 55 kg. The emu cannot fly but it can run up to 50 kph! It's breeding time is from April to November when it lays six to eight green and speckled eggs. The emu builds its nest out of stones and grass in the shape of a circle.

Back to A-Z Home Page

There is a picture and description about each of the animals. Your students could start a virtual zoo of animals on different continents by utilizing some of the graphics here.

This Web site also has information about exploring Australia and has a map section which would provide you with detail maps of some of the regions and cities. You will also find a Web page with the lyric to "Waltzing Matilda" and sound files for both it and the National Anthem, "Advance Australia Fair."

Lone Pine Koala Sanctuary

Koalas at Lone Pine Koala Sanctuary
Copyright © 1997 Lone Pine Koala Sanctuary. All rights reserved.
http://www.koala.net/

 This Koala will greet you as you enter the Lone Pine Koala Sanctuary. You are invited to take a virtual tour of the sanctuary. The Web pages automatically move forward in this tour. You could download this, using the Site To Go utility and students could sit around the computer and watch without needing someone at the keyboard.

There is information about the animals in the sanctuary and they'll even send you a newsletter if you sign up for it.

The wildlife gallery is a large resource for photographs of many of the animals in Australia. These would be good illustrations for the students' virtual zoo or for a project in which each student makes a small poster about an animal living in Australia. You might have them create a book about these animals, laminate the pages, and present it to students in a younger grade to read.

If you use any of the photos from the wildlife gallery, please make sure you credit the sanctuary for the photographs. Along with the terrific photos in the virtual tour, you will find photos of koala, kangaroos, wallaby, possum, dingos, tasmanian devils, lizards, snakes, and birds.

More Than Meets The Eye

There is always more to see at Lone Pine Koala Sanctuary. With close to 100 species of Australian Native animals for you to get close to, a full day of experiences will greet you.

Copyright c 1997 Lone Pine Koala Sanctuary. All rights reserved.

Other Australia Web Sites:

About: Australia
http://www.ozramp.net.au/~senani/austral.htm

About: The Outback
http://www.ozramp.net.au/~senani/outback.htm

About Australia!
http://www.about-australia.com/about.htm

Travelling Australia—On the Internet
http://www.travelaus.com.au/

Australia in Brief
http://www.dfat.gov.au/ipb/aust_brief_96/

Image Disk Photography
(digital photos of Australia that students can use in projects)
http://www.imagedisk.com.au/welcome1.html

Cuddly Koala's My World
http://www.effect.net.au/cuddlyK/myworld/myworld.html

The Australian Online
http://www.australian.aust.com/

The Age—Melbourne Online
http://www.theage.com.au/

Larry's Aussie Slang and Phrase Dictionary
http://www.uq.net.au/~zzlreid/slang.html

Koala Net
(rock & traditional sound files of Waltzing Matilda, slang dictionary,
and photographs)
http://www.w2d.com/koala-net/index.htm?intro

True Blue Aussie Slang Source
http://mail.enternet.com.au/~goeldner/test3c.htm

Australian Currency
(graphics showing examples of their currency)
http://xray.sai.msu.su/~mystery/images/money/AU/

Royal Australian Mint
(information about how coins are produced)
http://www.ramint.gov.au/

The Perth Mint
(coins with photography of animals, etc. featured on the coins)
http://www.perthmint.com/index.html

PHARAOHS, PYRAMIDS, AND PAPYRUS

Travel back in time and take your students on a virtual tour of ancient Egypt. Visit the tombs of pharaohs, travel down the River Nile, see treasures of lost empires, and write about your journey on papyrus. These are all things your students can do with the help of the Internet and some terrific Web sites.

The Tomb of the Chihuahua Pharaohs

At first glance, this Web site looks like it would be a satire of the pharaohs of ancient Egypt, but it is really the creation of Science and Social Studies teacher Kevin Fleury.

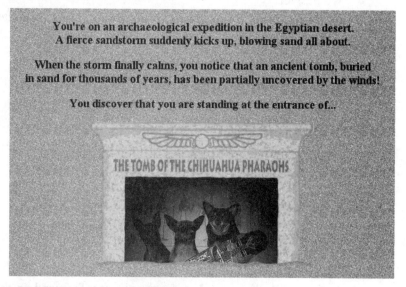

You're on an archaeological expedition in the Egyptian desert. A fierce sandstorm suddenly kicks up, blowing sand all about.

When the storm finally calms, you notice that an ancient tomb, buried in sand for thousands of years, has been partially uncovered by the winds!

You discover that you are standing at the entrance of...

THE TOMB OF THE CHIHUAHUA PHARAOHS

The Tomb of the Chihuahua Pharaohs
http://members.aol.com/crakkrjack/egypt.html

Take a second glance inside as Neferchichi, Neferkiki, and Corkankhamun take you on a tour of Egypt. You will find information about the history of ancient Egypt, graphics that your students can use in research projects, and lessons for you to incorporate in your unit plan.

Neferchichi will share her favorite graphics with you. This section includes photographs of statues, sphinxes, and other artifacts in these categories:

Gods & Goddesses
King Tut Artifacts
Amulets & Jewelry
Statues & Reliefs
Pyramids & Sphinxes
Mummy Stuff
Paintings & Imagery

Print copies of the graphics and create a bulletin board with a large pyramid on it. Put the graphics (artifacts) in several different chambers deep inside your pyramid and have the students identify the artifacts from this archeological excursion. You might want to number the artifacts so they can keep a record of which ones they have identified.

Use the Site To Go utility to download the graphics pages and the lesson ideas. Students could also create Web pages or multimedia presentations to explain about some of the artifacts in the graphics. There are many from which to choose. Once you have downloaded the graphics, you should be able to import them into a word processing document as well.

Corkankhamun will take you on a tour of how mummies are made both in Egypt and in other ancient civilizations. You will even find some lesson plans for making mummies from oranges or a chicken.

If you or your students have any questions about Egypt or you have any lesson plans or activities that you'd like to share, you are invited to e-mail Kevin at crakkrjack@aol.com. He will answer questions and will add your lesson ideas to those posted at his Web site.

Tour Egypt

Sponsored by Egypt's Ministry of Tourism (The Egyptian Tourist Authority), this Web site has information about contemporary Egypt as well as historical information for student research. The "Destinations in Egypt" section has information about the different areas in Egypt. There are photographs of many tourist attractions such as pyramids and sphinxes.

You are the 1804387 visitor since Dec. 29th, 1996 to the

Official Internet Site of:

The Ministry of Tourism, Egypt
The Egyptian Tourist Authority

The Egyptian Tourism Ministry wishes you a warm welcome to the Country of Egypt, and to Misr. Please take a moment to meet the President of Egypt and read the introduction by the Egyptian Minister of Tourism. We have a vast on-line resource about Egypt, which we constantly update. Bookmark Tour Egypt.

Music | Bulletins from the Ministry

About Egypt
A brief invitation to Egypt

What's New
New additions to Tour Egypt

The Egypt BBS
Online discussions about Egypt

Subscribe to Our Newsletter
Keep in touch with Egypt

Ministry of Tourism   E T A
The Official Seals

Tour Egypt
http://touregypt.net/

Each location featured at this Web site has links for "About the Area," "The Past," "Travel and Fun," "Sights to See," and "Maps of the Area." The featured areas include:

Alexandria	Aswan and Nubia	Cairo	Luxor
Red Sea	Sinai	The Delta	

Your students will also enjoy the "Color Me Egypt—Just For Kids" section. There is an illustrated history of Egypt that you can download using the Site To Go utility. They will see photographs of pyramids, hieroglyphics, and the Nile River.

The "Color Me Egypt: Just For Kids" section also has a contest for children to enter. Children ages 7–12 can draw or paint pictures of

Egyptian scenes or artifacts while younger children can color the coloring pages provided at the Web site. They can then send them in for judging and win prizes.

A painting of Osiris that is located in the Tomb of Sinnedjem, who was in charge of decorating the tombs of the kings and queens.

This painting of Amun-Re, Ramesses II and Mut is located in the temple Abu Simbel.

These are some samples of the coloring pages at this Web site. Be sure to download them all and have your younger students color them or take them home as a fun activity.

There is a section of the site which has graphics of the flag and an emblem for downloading to use with projects.

At "Wild Egypt," you can take your students on an online safari. This is another virtual tour of wildlife of a particular region of the world. Your students could use the graphics and information found here as part of a virtual zoo project featuring animals of different continents of the world.

The online safaris include A Nile Journey, An Over-Land Adventure, and A Red Sea Dive. You can use these in a Social Studies lesson about different regions of the world or in a Science lesson about different habitats.

Egypt's Tourism Net

Egypt Tourism Net
http://www.idsc.gov.eg/tourism/index.htm

This Web site has a section called "Tourist Attractions," which has quite a few photographs that could be used in student projects. However, the frame structure for this site makes it difficult for *Web Buddy* to download the Web pages and graphics if you follow the link on the index page. If you go to this URL:

http://www.idsc.gov.eg/cgi-win/pinfo1f.exe/1

you should have no problem downloading that section of the Web site using the Site To Go utility.

Once downloaded, this is another example of a virtual tour of a country. You could also print these pages, or parts of them, on overhead transparency film. Be sure to use inkjet or deskjet transparency film and set your printer settings to transparency so you have enough ink on them. Use them as part of your instructional materials about Egypt.

Page 1 out of 6 pages (each page has up to 20 record)

Abydos

* **Place Address:** Suhag, Egypt
* **Place kind:** Pharaonic

Agilika Island

* **Place Address:** Aswan, Egypt
* **Place kind:** Island

Agricultural Museum

* **Place Address:** Dokki, Giza
  Tel:+20-2-3608682/1
* **Place kind:** Museum

Egyptian Tourism Net—Tourist Attractions
http://www.idsc.gov.eg/cgi-win/pinfo1f.exe/1

Egyptian Projects

Now—if you're wondering what your students can do with all this information, look at what Ms. Hos-McGrane's students did. They have completed projects about many ancient civilizations including Rome, China, Vikings, Celts, Maoris, and Incas.

You can connect to those projects and this one about Ancient Egypt from the index page. These are students in grade six at the International School of Amsterdam. They spent a month working on their study of Egypt and created multimedia projects to show other students. Several of the projects are now being shared with students around the world by being posted at their Web site. There are also some links to other projects about Egypt which are online at other Web sites.

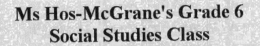

Ms Hos-McGrane's Grade 6 Social Studies Class

Welcome to our Ancient History Project Pages

Based on a lithograph
"Side View of the Great Sphinx, Pyramids of Geezeh"
by David Roberts , 1838

Ms Hos-McGrane's Grade 6 Social Studies Class
http://www.xs4all.nl/~swanson/origins/eg_history_intro.html

The River Nile ▶

The Ancient Egyptians depended on the Nile itself. If there was much rain they were saved almost by a miracle. they would depend on the flooding of the Nile to cover and enrich their crops; once the water went back to its normal size it would leave a layer of fertile black mud. It would usually flood in August. The Ancient Egptians thought the flood was given by their gods.

Honoring a god was very important, so when a flood came they would thank Hapi,, the Nile god. They thought that if they did not express their gratitude the gods might not send the flood again. Most peasants built their houses on mounds above the flood level and moved their animals to higher ground as the Nile rose.

The Nile brought many gifts such as papyrus which they needed to make paper. It is a green pland that is cut with fine knives to make the strips. Then the strips are laid out in two layers and a cover is put over it. Then a rock is used to beat the papyrus plant. Finally the cover is taken off and the papyrus is left to

Egyptian Projects—Sample Screen
http://www.xs4all.nl/~swanson/origins/egyptintro.html

Other Egypt Web Sites:

NOVA Online—Pyramids—The Inside Story
http://www.pbs.org/wgbh/nova/pyramid/

Focus on Egypt
http://www.focusmm.com/egypt/eg_anamn.htm

Map of Egypt
http://www.focusmm.com/egypt/eg_map.htm

Ancient Egypt Project—Internet lesson plan
http://www.teleport.com/community/schools/Milwaukie_HS/Inter net_Lesson_Plans/egypt/anc_egypt.html

Nefertiti
http://www.malone.org/~jrodrigu/isis/queen.html

Die Like an Egyptian—student project guidelines & teacher's guide
http://207.63.217.2/enternet97/projects/egypt/egypt2.htm

Carnegie Museum of Natural History—Life in Ancient Egypt
http://www.clpgh.org/cmnh/tours/egypt/

Teacher's Guide to The Walton Hall of Ancient Egypt
http://www.clpgh.org/cmnh/tours/egypt/guide.html

Newton's Apple—Mummies
http://www.ktca.org/newtons/13/mummy.html

GEOGRAPHY LESSON PLANS

There are many great lesson plans being posted on the Internet but you probably don't have time to sit and read them while you are online. *Web Buddy* is the perfect solution to that problem. This lesson takes a look at Geography and Social Studies "lesson banks" online.

Florida Geographic Alliance

FGA Summer Institute in Russia!!!

About FGA
Look here for more information about the Florida Geographic Alliance, including how to get in touch with our staff and TC's.

Registration
If you would like to register online to become a member of the Florida Geographic Alliance, this section is for you

Lesson Plans
Here you will find a gold mine of lesson plans free for use in your classroom. Please give credit to the authoring teacher(s) when applicable.

Outline Maps
FGA has a growing collection of outline maps avalable in Adobe Acrobat format. They are sorted by continent

Florida Geographic Alliance
http://multimedia2.freac.fsu.edu/fga/index.html

This Web site has geography lesson plans from teachers who have attended summer institute programs.

Lesson plans from the Florida Educational Technology and Leadership Institute include such topics as:

> Native American Populations
> Outback Down Under
> Railroads, Cities, and Industry
> Lewis and Clark's Expedition to the Northwest
> Agriculture, Communication, and Time
> North America: U.S. Neighbors

Lesson plans from the 1997 Summer Institute include:

> Biomes
> Historic Cemeteries
> Physical Geography
> Global Communities
> Indo-European Language Family
> Physically Featured
> Writing in Geography

FGA Lesson Plans

These lesson plans are made available to you free of cost. Use them as you wish, but please give credit to the author(s) where applicable

- Florida Education Technology and Leadership Institute *(8)*
- Summer 1997 Lesson Plans *in Progress*
- Summer 1995 Lesson Plans *(21)*
- Summer 1994 Lesson Plans *(43)*
- Summer 1993 Lesson Plans *(12)*
- Florida's History Through Its Places *(20)*
- Geography Academy for Teachers Units *(30)*
- Miscellaneous Lesson Plans *(23)*

There are more lessons from previous years on file at this site. The lessons are available for teachers to download and use. You can use the Site To Go utility to download an entire set and then read them while you are offline.

The Alliance has also provided maps in Adobe Acrobat 3.0 format for teachers to download and use in their classrooms. There is an assortment of types of maps of Africa, Asia, Australia, and Europe.

If you don't have the Adobe Acrobat Reader program, there is a link on the page to download it. The Reader is a free program that allows you to read files in the .pdf format.

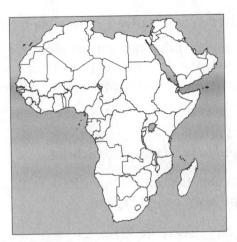

Sample Blank Outline Map of Africa

There are outline maps of continents and countries. You can download blank outline maps, maps with country names labeled, maps with major cities identified, landform maps, and maps showing the types of vegetation.

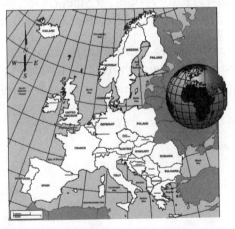

Sample Country Map of Europe

 Use the Site To Go utility to download the map index page and the linked map files, if you want the entire set. It will take a while to download all of the .pdf files into your temporary category. Then you can quickly save them all to disk by opening that Web page from your *Web Buddy* Central program, clicking on each hypertext link, and choosing to save each of the files.

Other Geography Lesson Web Sites:

Geography Education@nationalgeographic.com
(lesson, unit, and activity plans from teachers around the country)
**http://www.nationalgeographic.com/resources/ngo/education/ideas.
html**

Youth Net
http://yn.la.ca.us/welcome.html

Columbia Education Center Lesson Plans
http://www.col-ed.org/cur/

Internet Classroom Activities
http://www.dorsai.org/~jberger/Activitiesindex.html

Social Studies Resources—Kent, Washington
**http://www.kent.wednet.edu/curriculum/soc_studies/soc_studies.
html**

SCORE History—Social Science Resources
http://www.rims.k12.ca.us/SCORE/index.html

Marc Sheehan's Lesson Plans Page
(also has a collection of links to other lesson plan Web sites)
http://www.halcyon.com/marcs/lessons.html

CATERPILLARS TO BUTTERFLIES

Linking literature and science is easy when you're working with books like Eric Carle's *The Very Hungry Caterpillar* and animals like butterflies. You can use this book as a springboard for this unit, regardless of the age of your students. (Just remember—a butterfly forms a chrysalis; a moth forms a cocoon.)

Carrie Bruner's Thematic Unit

Carrie Bruner has created a Web page which gives examples of student work from her class unit about Eric Carle's book, *The Very Hungry Caterpillar*. Use the Page To Go utility to download this page and keep it as a teaching resource.

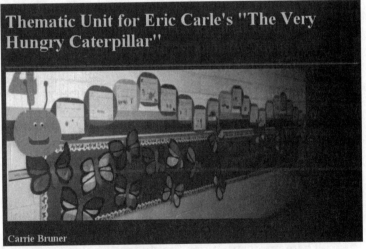

Thematic Unit for Eric Carle's "The Very Hungry Caterpillar"

Carrie Bruner

Carrie Bruner's Thematic Unit
http://members.aol.com/CBRUNER1/index.html

The large caterpillar has segments for the students' stories about what they would eat if they were very hungry caterpillars. They made butterflies from construction paper and colored tissue paper. The class constructed a pictograph illustrating their votes for favorite butterfly. Science played a big role as the students compared and contrasted butterflies and moths and studied mealworm development as another life cycle of an insect.

Monarch Watch

The Monarch Watch Web site has scientific information about Monarch butterflies and curriculum materials for grades K–8.

Monarch Watch
http://www.monarchwatch.org/

There is background information about the life cycle of butterflies and the migration of the Monarchs.

There are instructions for student-scientist partnership projects such as Tagging Monarchs. They have detailed how you would collect and tag the butterflies as they migrate through your region.

Milkweed is the exclusive food of the Monarch larvae. They have included a photo guide to various types of milkweed plants and instructions for creating a butterfly garden.

You could use the Site To Go utility to download several pages of information or a group of age-relative lesson plans and activities.

The activities are age-appropriate and include complete plans such as the following which teaches the basics of taxonomy by using the students' shoes.

K-2 Curriculum

Taxonomy & Butterfly Systematics

Classroom Activities

The two activities below introduce young students to different aspects of taxonomy.

Activity 1: Classifying Shoes

This is a great way to introduce the idea of classification to students! You can ham it up by talking about how disgusting all the shoes are, refusing to touch them, and moving them around with a meter stick. The students love it!

Procedure

1. Have each student take off one shoe and put it into a pile in the middle of the room.

2. Tell students that the class is going to sort the shoes into groups based on similarity or shared characteristics. Have them talk about ways to sort them. Let students choose the shoe categories, but set a ground rule that the categories must be value-free (e.g., sorting into ugly, boring, or cool categories is not OK). It is probably best not to let price be a category either.

3. Following the students' directions, sort the shoes by criteria the class chooses.

The Page To Go utility would work well for downloading one or two of the activity pages.

Use their FAQ (or Frequently Asked Questions) list as a scavenger hunt list for your class. The list includes questions such as:

- How much does a Monarch weigh?
- Do Monarchs occur outside of North America?
- How long do adult Monarchs live?
- Why do Monarchs have only 4 legs?

Write these and the other questions on the list on large construction paper butterflies. Have your students try to find the answers without looking at the Monarch Watch Web site.

The Butterfly Web Site

The Butterfly WebSite is an index of butterfly resources on the Internet. It also contains graphics of hundreds of butterflies, reports of butterfly watches worldwide, and information about attracting butterflies.

The education page has butterfly projects that students and teachers have described to them via e-mail. Your class could also e-mail them about your butterfly projects. They'll post them on the Web site.

 Use Page To Go to download the projects or graphics pages that interest you and your students.

The Butterfly WebSite
http://www.butterflyWeb site.com/

Some of the projects described here include:

- butterfly gardens—growing flowers butterflies feed on (some received grant money or assistance from local vendors)
- a butterfly atrium—a 2-story enclosure for raising butterflies and testing student-designed feeders
- rearing Monarchs from caterpillars for tagging and releasing— videotaping the stages—sending the tape to penpals

Butterflies of North America

Created and maintained by the Northern Prairie Wildlife Research Center near Jamestown, North Dakota, this site is an online guide to caterpillars and butterflies in North America. The research center is one of many science centers operated by the Biological Resources Division of the U.S. Geological Survey, which is a bureau of the U.S. Department of the Interior.

≋USGS   Northern Prairie Wildlife
                                             Research Center

Butterflies of North America

North America Distribution Maps
    Photos, species accounts, and combined maps for butterflies ocurring in the conterminous U.S. and
    northern Mexico

Northern Prairie Wildlife Research Center Home Page
Paul A. Opler, Harry Pavulaan, and Ray E. Stanford
http://www.npwrc.org/resource/distr/lepid/bflyusa/bflyusa.htm

Choose your state from the map or the lists on the main Web page. Use the Site To Go utility to download the field guide for your state to use in your classroom as an identification key.

Each state Web page has a list of the butterflies found in that state and a link to a Web page about each butterfly. Many of the pages have photographs of the butterflies, caterpillars and chrysales. There is also biological data about many of the butterflies including life history, flight, habitat, caterpillar and butterfly food, and range.

≋USGS   Northern Prairie Wildlife
Research Center

Butterflies of North America

Butterflies of North Carolina

Eastern Tiger Swallowtail (*Papilio glaucus*)

Eastern Tiger Swallowtail   Caterpillar

Eastern Tiger Swallowtail (*Papilio glaucus* Linnaeus)

Wing span: 3 5/8 - 6 1/2 inches (9.2 - 16.5 cm)

Identification: Male is yellow with dark tiger stripes. Female has 2 forms: one yellow like the male and the other

Your students could choose a butterfly and find photographs and scientific information or graphics from other sites. They could then create a poster presentation about it or create a "Butterfly Wanted" poster including a picture and information about where the butterfly might be found and what it might be eating. Once you have the information from these sites on your computer, they can take time looking at the paintings and photographs and draw their own illustrations for their posters.

Other Butterfly Web Sites:

Eric Carle's Home Page
http://www.eric-carle.com/

CyberGuide—The Very Hungry Caterpillar
http://www.sdcoe.k12.ca.us/score/carle/carletg.html

Sequencing Activity—The Very Hungry Caterpillar
http://faldo.atmos.uiuc.edu/CLA/LESSONS/111.html

Caterpillars to Butterflies
http://ericir.syr.edu/Virtual/Lessons/Science/Biological/BIO0016.html

GOING BATTY

Comic book characters, movie cartoon characters, and Halloween critters that swoop down to get us—bats have gotten such a diverse reputation that maybe it's time to set the record straight.

There are quite a few resources online about bats (which are mammals belonging to the Order Chiroptera—meaning hand-wing). Let's look at a few which might offer some factual information and some ideas for a unit plan about bats.

Holy Bat Box Batman!

This Web site was created by Jim Buzbee, who decided to do some research about bats and try to figure out how to attract them to his yard. Several years and 2 bat houses later, he has a very informative Web site.

Holy Bat Box Batman!
it's The Buzbee Bat House Temperature Plot !

Do I have too much time on my hands or what ? I didn't think so, but how then do I explain this ?

It began one evening in Egypt several years ago. I was crossing the Nile on a small sailboat and was fascinated by the sight of bats skimming the surface of the river, snatching up the insects. Upon returning home to Denver, I thought it might be interesting to put up a bat house to see if I could attract any bats. After a couple of months of trying to convince my wife, she relented (and actually bought me a book on bats). So my Son and I built and erected the bat house.

Now after two years of waiting, (much to my wife's relief and my daughter's dismay) no bats. So I read up on the known habits of bats and made a few changes. I moved the house a bit, and caulked and painted it. It turns out that one of the most important factors for a bat when selecting a place to roost, is the temperature. So I decided to see what was happening inside, and share this important information with the world. Thus this page. The most current temperature is on the right and is sampled every half hour. The image represents a span of approximately 5 days.

UPDATE 06/04/97 : Well, the two years in the above paragraph have stretched to four, but I'm not giving up ! I signed up with Bat Conservation International's North American Bat House Research Project, and ordered the

The Buzbee Bat House Temperature Plot
http://www.nyx.net/~jbuzbee/bat_house.html

You might want to follow his suggestions and order or build a bat house at your school to see if you can attract any of the insect-eating mammals.

Be aware that there are quite a few links to other Web sites. You may simply want to use the Page To Go utility to download his page as an index page for your students to use if they are searching while online.

Kindergarten Lesson Plans

Sherrye Chapman's Web site has a page devoted to lesson plans which she has used with her classes. The Web page starts with ideas to use with Janell Cannon's book, *Stellaluna*.

Kindergarten Lesson Plans

I hope you enjoy these lesson plans. These are lesson plans or units that actually work with a classroom full of kids and one teacher!

Bats- This lesson plan focuses on the book *Stellaluna*.

This lesson plan will serve to dispell many myths about bats and teach children about the good things that bats do. I spent one week on this unit. It may be extended for a longer period of time.

   Vocabulary: nocturnal, vampire, mammal

Activity 1: Introduce the unit with a KWL chart about bats. Read *Bats-Creatures of the Night* by Joyce Milton.

For the KWL chart, I drew three poster size bats in different poses and colored them with chalks. I laminated the pictures. One bat poster is the K poster. Let the children tell you everything they Know about bats. Be sure to include misinformation. This will be cleared up later. The second poster is the W poster. Let the kids ask questions about things they Want to know about bats. Steer them towards appropriate questions if necessary. The third part of the chart, the L chart, will not be done until the end of the unit. The L chart is where the kids

Kindergarten Lesson Plans
http://seaesc2.sesc.k12.ar.us/hamburg/lessonplans.htm

You can use the Page To Go utility to download this Web page of lesson ideas for use in your classroom.

Bats of Arizona

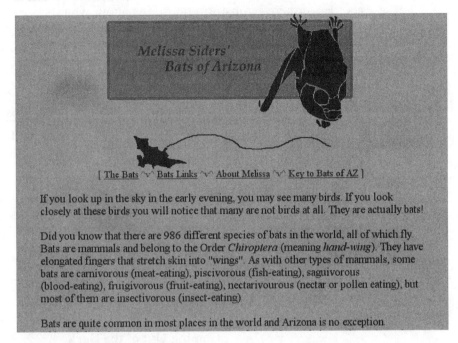

[The Bats ⌄ Bats Links ⌄ About Melissa ⌄ Key to Bats of AZ]

If you look up in the sky in the early evening, you may see many birds. If you look closely at these birds you will notice that many are not birds at all. They are actually bats!

Did you know that there are 986 different species of bats in the world, all of which fly. Bats are mammals and belong to the Order *Chiroptera* (meaning *hand-wing*). They have elongated fingers that stretch skin into "wings". As with other types of mammals, some bats are carnivorous (meat-eating), piscivorous (fish-eating), saguivorous (blood-eating), fruigivorous (fruit-eating), nectarivourous (nectar or pollen eating), but most of them are insectivorous (insect-eating)

Bats are quite common in most places in the world and Arizona is no exception.

Bats of Arizona
http://www.xpressWeb.com/~talon/BATSinAZ.html

This site was created by Melissa Siders and David Sinton. Melissa is a Wildlife Biologist for the U. S. Forest Service in Arizona. Together, they have created a Web site with information about a wide variety of bats. They are sorted by type as well as a dichotomous key for identifying the bats found in Arizona.

You could use the Site To Go utility to download several Web sites about bats and have your students compare what they have heard about bats with what is actually true.

Create a large KWL chart to hang on your wall. Start your lesson by having your students tell you what they already Know about bats. Write all their suggestions in the K column (whether they are factual or not).

Then have your students tell you what they Want to Know about bats. Have them brainstorm questions about what bats eat, where they might live, whether they attack people, and even whether they turn into vampires or talk like the cartoon characters in movies. The level of questioning will change depending on the age of the students. Write all their questions in the W column.

Have the students work individually or in teams to research through the various Web sites you have downloaded or use the index from the Buzbee Web site to locate the answers to all their questions. Have them write the answers as they find them in the L column to signify that this is something they have Learned about bats.

Oklahoma Bats

You should also visit this Web site, maintained by the Northern Prairie Wildlife Research Center, about bats in Oklahoma.

Oklahoma Bats

. . . Coming Out of the Dark

Nongame Wildlife Program
Oklahoma Department of Wildlife Conservation
1801 N. Lincoln.
Oklahoma City, OK 73105
(405)521-4616

Introduction

Bats are the only flying mammals. The bones in a bat's wing are the same as those of the human arm and hand.

Oklahoma Bats—Coming out of the Dark
http://www.npsc.nbs.gov/resource/othrdata/okbats/okbats.htm

In addition to having instructions online for building your own bat house, they have a list of bat trivia questions which you may want to use as starter questions for your students to research. You can use the Page To Go utility to download this page with the answers to questions such as:

- Do bats lay eggs?
- Are bats blind?
- Are bats dangerous?

You could also use the Site To Go utility to download the entire site and use it as reference material for research projects.

Other Stellaluna and Bats Web Sites:

Janell Cannon—author of *Stellaluna*
http://www.friend.ly.net/user-homepages/j/jorban/scoop/biographies/jcannon.html

Bat Thematic Unit
http://www.cccoe.k12.ca.us/bats/welcome.html

Teacher View—review and lesson ideas—*Stellaluna*
http://www.eduplace.com/tview/tviews/lojas5.html

We're Going Batty—WebQuest
http://www.lfelem.lfc.edu/tech/DuBose/Webquest/schaffner/bats.html

Bat Facts and Amazing Trivia—Bat Conservation International
http://www.batcon.org/trivia.html

Bats and You
http://dnr.state.il.us/ildnr/offices/nat_her/bats/bats.htm

BIG, BAD WOLVES?

Through stories such as Little Red Riding Hood, Lon Po Po, Peter and the Wolf, and The Three Little Pigs, literature has "taught" us that wolves are fearsome creatures that will hunt us down and most likely "wolf us down."

Some other stories which you could use to begin your unit about wolves have attempted to set the story straight. These include, but are not limited to:

- *The True Story of the Three Little Pigs* by Jon Scieszka
- *Julie of the Wolves* by Jean Craighead-George
- *Never Cry Wolf* by Farley Mowat

Another story you could use is online at the Jack London Collection Web site. Part of his book, *Love of Life & Other Stories,* "Brown Wolf" is a story about a pet wolf. This story and almost all his work is online in complete form at this Web site.

The Jack London Collection
http://sunsite.Berkeley.EDU/London/

You could download just the "Brown Wolf" story at this URL:

http://sunsite.berkeley.edu/London/Writings/LoveLife/wolf.html

by using the Page To Go utility. Or you could use the Convert utility to create a document you could use in your word processing program. This would be a wonderful story to share with your students.

Wolf Shadows—Mary Casanova

For older students, you might want to start your wolf unit by reading all or part of *Wolf Shadows*. This should spark a good discussion of how people and wolves should interact. Mary could also be an "Author of the Month" in your classroom. Use the information at her Web site to generate interest in her books.

Children's Author

Hi! I'm Mary Casanova, and I write books for kids of all ages (from 7 to 97). I live "up north" along the Minnesota-Canadian border. Often, when I'm hiking or cross-country skiing, I come across the tracks of moose and wolves. More than once I've spotted a wolf crossing a remote road or frozen lake. I hope you'll discover a bit of this wilderness in some of my books.

My home page is a good way to keep in touch with you. I'll update it often, sharing bits and pieces of news, the stories behind my stories, and what's happening with my books. I hope you'll visit frequently. If you have comments or questions, feel free to e-mail me. I'd love to hear from you!

Mary Casanova
http://www.marycasanova.com/

Mary lives in Minnesota near the Canadian border and shares that wilderness and its wildlife through her books.

The song started low, a single voice rising, then was quickly joined by a chorus of high-pitched and thoatier howls. The song rose and fell, traveling over the treet...

When Seth hears wolves howling in the woods behind his home, it sends a chill down his spine. Even though he can't help the unreasoning fear that creeps over him, Seth wants to see the wolf packs thrive.

But Seth's beliefs put him at odds with those who want to hunt wolves again. Seth's best friend, Matt, among them. It seems to Seth he is being forced to choose between wolves and a lifelong friendship-and then Matt commits an irrational act of violence . . .

Coming in August!

Cover Illustration © 1997 Dan Brown

WOLF SHADOWS

THE STORY BEHIND THE STORY

One day, when skiing through the woods, I came across a fresh wolf kill. The snow was stained red. Tawny fur was scattered over wolf and deer tracks. Only a few small bones remained. The wolves had wasted nothing

I've long held a fascination for wolves. Every time I see a wolf crossing a remote road or see one traveling across a frozen lake, I'm filled with awe and wonder. I'm glad to see the wolf population thrive, but not everyone feels as I do.

Literature alone, however, is not going to teach children about wolves as wild creatures. There are, however, some organizations throughout the country with educational resources available at their Web sites to help you teach your students.

Wolf Haven International

Wolf Haven International
http://www.teleport.com/~wnorton/wolf.shtml

Once this Web page opens, you will hear a haunting wolf howl. Once you download these pages, using the Site To Go utility, you can take this information to your students. Start your lesson by opening that page on your computer and get everyone's attention.

There are photographs of wolves, other sound files, bio-sheets about all the wolves that are residents at Wolf Haven, and information about their adoption program.

What is a Wolf?

What is a wolf?

A wolf is a large predator that depends for its survival on large prey, such as deer, elk, caribou, and in some parts of its range, moose and bison that tip the scales at more than a thousand pounds. It has powerful jaws capable of exerting about 1500 pounds per square inch, or about twice that of the domestic dog. It is accustomed to a feast and famine existence, often going many days without eating then gorging as much as 20 pounds in a single sitting. It's role in nature is to remove the sick and the weak, and in this way create a win-win relationship with its prey. The end result is a system which has succeeded for hundreds of thousands of years.

The wolf is a highly social animal, generally living within the same pack for most, if not all, of its life. Survival depends very much upon the pack. The members of the pack cooperate in hunting, killing large prey, feeding and caring for the young, defending their territory against other packs, and so forth. The pack functions mostly as a strong autocratic system, with each individual having fought for its placement or rank within the group. Generally only the top male and female are permitted to breed, while any attempts to do so by others are punished. When to hunt, where to hunt, and many other activities are also commonly determined by the pack leaders.

Most packs occupy a range of about 80 to 100 square miles, and move about it on a regular basis. The pack

The Wolf Haven site is also a good place to start if you're looking for a general information page about what wolves are. You can download this with the Page To Go utility and add to a collection for student reference.

The Searching Wolf

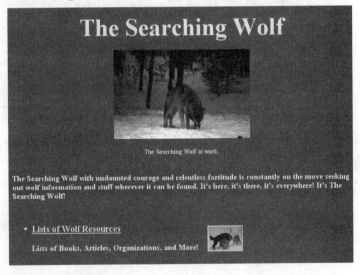

The Searching Wolf
http://www.iup.edu/%7Ewolf/wolves.htmlx

Dr. Bill Forbes, Professor of Biology at Indiana University of Pennsylvania, is the creator of this Web site. It is with his assistance that the Searching Wolf has been able to find all these resources and bring them to the public eye.

There are photographs of wolves that your students could use in multimedia projects. They can even play sound files of howls and growls and learn techniques for howling. The photographs of a wolf skull, which is used as a teaching tool at the university, are incredible.

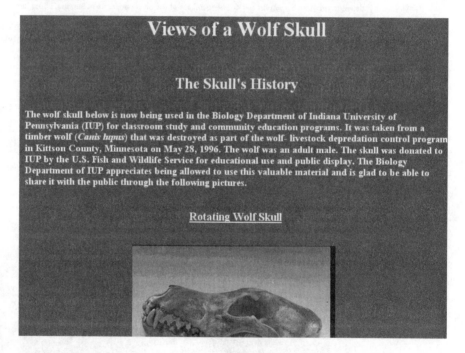

Views of a Wolf Skull

The Skull's History

The wolf skull below is now being used in the Biology Department of Indiana University of Pennsylvania (IUP) for classroom study and community education programs. It was taken from a timber wolf (*Canis lupus*) that was destroyed as part of the wolf- livestock depredation control program in Kittson County, Minnesota on May 28, 1996. The wolf was an adult male. The skull was donated to IUP by the U.S. Fish and Wildlife Service for educational use and public display. The Biology Department of IUP appreciates being allowed to use this valuable material and is glad to be able to share it with the public through the following pictures.

Rotating Wolf Skull

The photographs show all sides of the skull and there is also a moving graphic that shows the skull being rotated. Once you have downloaded these pages using the Site To Go utility, you will have a valuable teaching tool to use with your students to teach about wolves and canines in general or to teach about skulls.

My Wolf Page

"Lydius Wolf" has compiled several pages of wolf information into this Web site and has also provided some links to other sites about wolves, as well. These would provide background information for students about different types of wolves such as the Red, Alaskan, Mexican, Timber, Gray, and Maned.

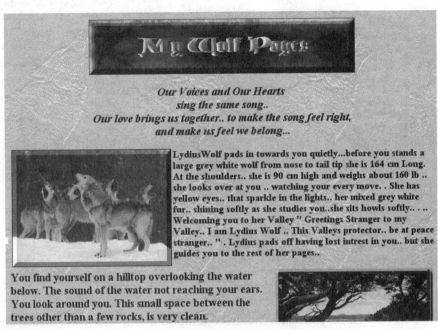

Welcome to My Wolf Spirit Pages—"Lydius Wolf"
http://mysterious.simplenet.com/wolf/

There is also information about what wolves are and what wolf packs are. This would be a great site to download with the Site To Go utility.

Your students could print the photographs and create posters about the different types of wolves by using this information and photographs from several of these Web sites. They could also use the graphics and various sound files in presentations by using software such as *HyperStudio*.

Timber Wolf Information Network Interactive

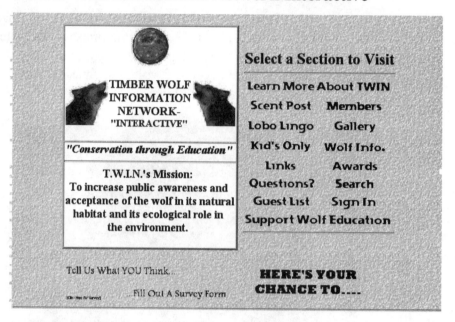

Timber Wolf Information Network Interactive
http://www.timberwolfinformation.org/

This Web site has a section geared toward educating students about wolves. They also post children's stories and artwork about wolves. Once your students have learned about wolves from the information on these Web sites, you could have them draw pictures or write stories of their own to submit to have them posted online.

If you have access to a scanner, you could scan their drawings and create a Web site of your own with student work. This would be a great way for your students to educate others about wolves. Add those stories to your school's Web site and start by educating other students in your school.

International Wolf Center

This Web site also has an archive of photographs of wolves and sound files of howls which your students could use in presentations and research papers.

Welcome to the International Wolf Center

People conserve only what they learn to understand and respect. That's why the International Wolf Center's mission focuses on education.

At the Center, we teach that wolves howl to communicate with each other, not with the moon. We use the language of predator and prey, of dominance and submission, of play postures and scent-marking to make the wolf real.

We believe that the more you learn about the real wolf - puppy fur, snowshoe paws, sharp teeth, and all - the better decisions you can make in support of the wolf's survival.

So learn. Then teach the next person. The stewardship of wolves around the world rests in the hearts, heads

International Wolf Center
http://www.wolf.org/

This is another good source for photographs of wolves and sound files of wolf howls. It also has educational information about wolves and has articles with current information about the status of wolves in the wild and their interactions with man. You could use the Site To Go utility to download these pages and have easy access to them on your computer, for your students to use in their projects.

Another project you might want to work on is a telemetry study. The scientists at the center keep track of several different wolves by radio telelmetry. The center will send you a map of the area (for a small fee) and you can download the telemetry data on a weekly basis and have teams of students in your class track different wolves. The data can be downloaded for months past as well so that you will have some background information about each of the wolves. They have also posted information about the specific wolves, including their names, so that each of your teams can learn a bit more about its wolf.

Other Wolf Web Sites:

Wolves, Wolves, and More Wolves
http://www.erols.com/redwolf/wolves.htm

Sarah Harrison's Wolf Page
http://albrecht.ecn.purdue.edu/~harrison/Wolf.html

Wolf Song of Alaska
http://www.alaska.net/~wolfsong/

Graywolf's Wolflink Page
http://www.graywolf.org/wolf.html

The Wolf Education & Research Center
http://www.wolfcenter.org/

International Wildlife Education & Conservation
http://www.iwec.org/Kits/wolf.html

CREATURES OF THE NIGHT

Nocturnal animals are those creatures which roam the fields, woods, and deserts while most of us are sleeping. What do they look like? What animals are they? How do they see at night? What do they eat?

This lesson will lead you to some resources that will introduce your students and you to some new animals and maybe teach you some things about animals you already know.

The Night Critters Page

Let's start this lesson with an idea of what you can do for your students. Created by Keri Lesyk for her First Grade students, this Web page is a clickable learning page about a few animals who are active at night.

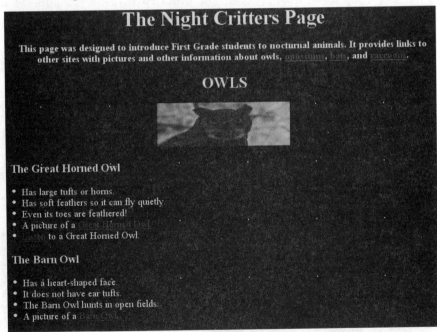

The Night Critters Page
http://grove.ufl.edu/~klesyk/night.html

It tells the students some information about owls, opossums, bats, and raccoons. There are links to other Web pages and sound files, such as owl cries. This would be a good project for you to create once you used the Site To Go utility to download several other Web sites. You might want to give more information for older students or you may just want to provide links to some pages you have downloaded.

Once you have sound files, graphics, and movie or animation files downloaded to your computer, these pages will load much more quickly. You could create a multimedia presentation for teaching your class about several of these animals.

Galagos and Lemurs

This is a small but informative Web page about Galagos, or Bushbabies, and Lemurs. The pictures to the upper left and lower right are Bushbabies. The other two wide-eyed animals are Lemurs. This would be a good page to add to a collection of pages about nocturnal animals by downloading with the Page To Go utility.

Galagos and Lemurs
http://www.algonet.se/~magnusbo/galago.html

Koalas at Lone Pine Koala Sanctuary

Koalas

The koala is unique to Australia and belongs to a group of mammals called marsupials that carry their young in a pouch on their abdomen. They live almost exclusively on a diet of eucalypt leaves.

Koalas do not get intoxicated from gum leaves. The koalas' relaxed lifestyle is an adaptation to the low energy content of the leaves. By moving slowly and resting or sleeping for up to 19 hours each day, koalas can conserve their energy.

In recent years, some wild koala populations have suffered a loss of numbers because man's development is encroaching on their habitat. Forest clearing for development, agriculture and industry has made the koala's food supply increasingly fragmented and scarce.

More than two million koalas were killed for their skins between 1908 and 1927. It has now been estimated that there are now 20,000 to 80,000 koalas in the wild.

A koala's tightly-packed fur repels water and provides the koala with better insulation that the fur of any other marsupial.

Koalas have few natural predators but can fall prey to dingoes. Occasionally young koalas are taken by goannas, wedge-tailed eagles and powerful owls.

Close to human settlement however, the greatest dangers to koala populations are the destruction of

Koalas at Lone Pine Koala Sanctuary
http://www.koala.net/

To conserve energy, the Koala is only awake a few hours each night to feed on eucalyptus leaves. The Koala Sanctuary Web site has information about Koalas, Wombats, and Possums, all nocturnal animals.

 You can add these pages to your class collection using the Page To Go option. Your students can then access these pages while you are studying nocturnal animals or during a study of Australia.

 These Web pages are also a good example of how your students can create Web pages with reports about other creatures of the night. They are designed with simple graphics and text.

South Yorkshire Badger Group

Welcome to the Home Page of the

South Yorkshire Badger Group

Reg. Charity No: 1039884

Hot Links

Last Update 25th July 1997

Badger Helpline 0378 660065

Introduction

The European Badger (*Meles Meles*) is one of Britains largest & possibly best loved wild mammal. With their distinctive black & white striped faces & shy gentle nature they certainly hold appeal for most people, yet few will have been lucky enough to have actually seen a badger in natural surroundings. This is because the Badger is a nocturnal animal which is normally secretive & tries to avoid man.

South Yorkshire Badger Group
http://www.shu.ac.uk/city/community/badger_group/

The Badger, another night creature, is one of Britain's most-loved mammals. It is a quiet animal which tends to stay away from people. This Web page gives you some information about the Badger and about efforts being made to preserve its population.

The site also has a Japanese Folk Tale, "The Teapot Badger," which you can share with your students. It is a story about a magic teapot which would turn into a snarling Badger whenever anyone tried to hurt it. Use the Site To Go utility to download both the information page and the folk tale.

The Arachnology Home Page

This Web site provides information about a variety of spiders. The site is from Belgium and most of the information is about spiders of Belgium. There are many links to other Web sites about spiders. There are also Web pages at this site with songs and sound files about spiders, stories and folk tales, and a page of links for children.

Welcome to

THE ARACHNOLOGY HOME PAGE

The Arachnological Hub of the World Wide Web

a repository and directory of arachnological information on the Internet

With millions of pages on the WWW it is difficult to find interesting arachnid related sites.
Therefore The Arachnology Home Page with already more than 1000 links to arachnological sites is an essential index to find quickly what you are looking for.
If you've got a site dealing with arachnids you can do two things to help others who are searching for information:
    1) send us your URL so we can include it in The Arachnology Home Page
    2) put a link to this page so visitors to your page find their way to our index

Arachnology Home Page
http://www.ufsia.ac.be/Arachnology/Arachnology.html

- Why does the black widow spider eat her mate? Coastal and Marine Institute, San Diego State University (USA)
- Thinking Fountain. Science Museum of Minnesota (USA) : Is a spider an insect? and Make a spider glider
- Teaching About Spiders, Spiders--Teacher Resource and Tarantulas The South Central Regional Technology in Education Consortium (USA)
- First Graders Learn About Spiders Briarcrest Elementary School (USA)
- The Smithsonian museums Resources and Tours Especially for Children (USA)
- The spider in the web (a child's story) Oliver Lesniak (8). Children's Art Foundation (USA)
- Minibeast World of Insects and Spiders BuzzWords: A Glossary of Arthropod Terms. Gary A. Dunn (USA)
- Chile Rose Tarantula Picture at the site of Lisa, a 12 year old girl from the United Kingdom
- Get this bug off of me! Daddy-long-legs, ticks, scorpions, black widow, brown recluse spider. Stephanie Bailey. University of Kentucky Entomology Department (USA)
- Itsy Bitsy Spiders Many primary grade students incorrectly identify spiders as insects. This web page is intended to be a resource to teachers and students in teaching and learning about the characteristics of spiders. Melinda Gulick. The University of South Carolina-Aiken (USA)
- Why don't spiders get caught in their own webs? You Can: Spider Webs. Jok Church (USA)
- Itsy and Bitsy Discuss Dinner Woodrow Wilson Leadership Program in Biology (USA)
- Tarantulas Get Real! Stories: Kids and Creatures (USA)

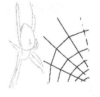

The children's link page has pages for and by students, stories written by children, photographs of spiders, and even some origami scorpion and spider instructions.

You could collect all the resources here by using the Site To Go utility. You would then have a large index of sites for your students to visit if your school does have online access.

Nocturnal animals must have well-developed eyesight or some other means of navigating at night. Here are a couple activities you could do with your students to illustrate how difficult it would be for us to suddenly become nocturnal animals.

Color Sorting Activity

Cut sets of different colored pieces of material into the same size square. Three or four inches should be a good size. The colors should be assorted in darks (blue, brown, black) and lights (pink, white, and yellow). Have a set of squares for several teams of students.

Have students start by making note of colors. Then have them attempt to sort them in the dark. Discuss how difficult it was.

Night Walk

Take a night walk in your classroom. Before the day of the walk, print about 20 different pictures from your collected Web pages. Mount them on cardboard or laminate so that you can re-use them. Get red cellophane to cover flashlights.

On the day of the walk, choose a location (multi-purpose room, media center, or classroom) and when the children are not in the room, tape the pictures in different places around the room. (With younger students, you would make them easier to find.)

Have students bring in flashlights from home and bring a few extras for those students (or pairs of students) who don't have one. Cover flashlights with red cellophane (so you don't startle the night creatures) and have the teams move around the room slowly and quietly to try to find all the hidden nocturnal animals.

Stop the activity about 10 minutes before the end of your class, turn on the lights, and point out where the animals were hidden.

Talk about taking night walks outside. Do your students think they could spot hidden nocturnal animals? Is being hidden important to the animals? Why?

Have your students access the Web pages you have downloaded and find out where those animals would hide in the wild. How does their hiding place help them find food? Other nocturnal animals your students might be familiar with include:

- cats
- porcupines
- scorpions
- wombats
- hedgehogs
- foxes
- mice
- bats

Add these to your collection of pictures of nocturnal animals for the night walk.

Other Nocturnal Animal Web Sites:

The Wonderful Skunk and Opossum Page
http://elvis.neep.wisc.edu/~firmiss/mephitis-didelphis.html

NOVA Online—Night Creatures of the Kalahari
(information and lesson plans & activities)
http://www.pbs.org/wgbh/nova/kalahari/

What are Prosimian Primates?
http://www.duke.edu/Web/primate/psimians.html

Scorpions
http://www.desertusa.com/oct96/du_scorpion.html

Eurasian Badgers
(a good site to download and use without his other pages or links)
http://homepages.enterprise.net/lemonhead/badger-2.htm

Wonderful World of Wombats
http://www.du.edu/~penrosel/wombat/index.html

Blue-Tongued Skinks
http://www.sonic.net/~melissk/bluetong.html

Martine Colette's Wildlife Waystation
http://www.waystation.org/animals/animals.html

Beach Mouse Info Page
http://www.ag.auburn.edu/~mwooten/main.html

Liska's EncycVulpedia (fox information)
http://www.telusplanet.net/public/foxstar/ev1con.htm

BITE INTO NUTRITION

Teeth, digestion, and good nutrition all play a vital role in our good health. Here are several Web sites which have teaching materials to help your students learn about their digestive system and how to take care of their teeth, the first step in the digestive process.

The Food Zone

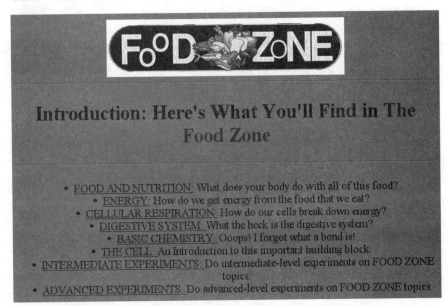

The Food Zone
http://kauai.cudenver.edu:3010/

With information about food and nutrition, energy, cells and cell function, and digestion, this Web site provides you with an entire teaching unit about food and nutrition. This resource was created by Dr. Gabriela Weaver and the University of Colorado at Denver. Please contact them before downloading from this site.

The digestive system is described as a "team" of body parts and organs that work within your body. There are tutorial lessons as well as experiments and activities you can do with your students.

The *1996* Digestive System Team.

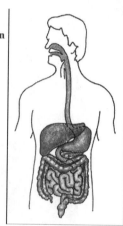

To meet any member of the team, click the organ directly on the diagram, or click the name below.

- The team roster:
  - ○ Oral Cavity "The Mouth"
  - ○ The Esophagus "The Squeeze"
  - ○ The Stomach "Churn and Burn"
  - ○ The Pancreas "The Source"
  - ○ The Liver "Vile Bile"
  - ○ The Small Intestine "The Long Haul"
  - ○ The Large Intestine "The Terminator"

The Digestive Team is divided into "members" and each is described in its own lesson section. You can use the Site To Go utility to download this tutorial. Then have students work together at the computer to find answers to scavenger hunt questions you have created.

The mouth is like a center on a football team. Everything starts right here. Nothing happens until food enters the mouth

The mouth has three not-so-secret weapons. Click on any of them to learn more about them!

- Teeth
- The Tongue
- The Salivary Glands.

The Mechanical and Chemical Parts of Digestion.

The teeth and tongue are involved in the mechanical parts of digestion. Digestion is considered to be mechanical when it does not change the general properties of the food. It is like building a table out of

You and your students will enjoy the "team" analogy as you read through the tutorial.

How do the teeth stay so tough and strong?

Like a running back, the teeth wear protective coating. The ***enamel*** covers the outside of the teeth is one of the hardest substances in the body. It is made of calcium salts. Enamel covers the teeth from the gums up

Why do we get tooth decay?

Bacteria, which are eaten with our food, cling on to the teeth. They eat away at the enamel of the teeth with acids and expose the insides of the teeth causing a tooth ache. If tooth decay gets really bad, then the tooth can die. Bacteria especially like to live off of sugars and carbohydrates, (Just like us, the bacteria prefer carbohydrates for cellular respiration which is why these foods are most likely to cause tooth decay.

But, the body has its own natural body guards, which help fight the bacteria. Saliva can help neutralize the acid of the bacteria, and keep the bacteria from getting through the enamel coating of the teeth.

The topics are thoroughly covered as shown in these screen shots from the "Digestive System Team," the oral cavity, and the teeth. You could set up this Web site on your computer and students could use it for review of topics they did not understand when you first presented them in class.

Your Gross & Cool Body

This Web site about the systems of the body and how they function is NOT for the faint-of-heart. Created by New Jersey Online, it discusses all those "gross" things kids want to know about like these and many more:

Bad Breath
Stomach Gurgles
Spit
Vomit
Hiccups
Ear Wax
Eye Gunk
Ankle Sprain

Your Gross & Cool Body
http://www.nj.com/yucky/body/

Wendell the Worm and Dora will lead your students to the answers to their "gross" questions about how their bodies work. They also investigate topics which include body systems and the senses.

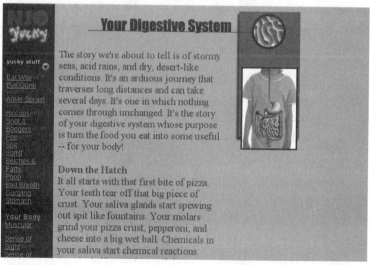

You can use the Site To Go utility to download most of the material here, but remember that things like the e-mail cards won't work offline.

Smiledoc

Drs. Kim Loos and R.K. Boyden
Family and Cosmetic Dentistry
1565 Hollenbeck Avenue, Suite 114
Sunnyvale, CA 94087, USA
Telephone: 408.736.4323

Fax: 408.736.9041

 WELCOME! THIS SITE IS UPDATED EVERY 30 DAYS. Our dental office received the **CONSUMER VALUESTAR AWARD** for outstanding patient satisfaction based on an independent survey. **View homepage in** Espanol, Deutsch, Japanese, Francais, Korean, Svenska, Chinese, or Italiano.

- WOW! Look What's New!
- Ask the Dentist-Searchable Weekly Updates!
- Meet the Dentists and Their Office Staff.
- Free Multimedia Dental Software for Children!
- Exclusive Articles by Distinguished Experts™.
- Experience Virtual Reality! Rotate a Tooth in 3-D Space
- Family Tips for a Better Smile™.
- About Our Dental Practice.
- Case Study Exemplars.
- Dental History from Gale Research Inc.

 CLICK HERE TO VISIT THE WORLD'S

Smiledoc
Drs. Kim Loos and R. K. Boyden
http://www.smiledoc.com/

Who better to teach about the importance of teeth as part of the digestive system than dentists? That's what these two dentists obviously decided when they created this Web site. There is information about keeping your teeth healthy and some fun things for students to do while they're visiting the site.

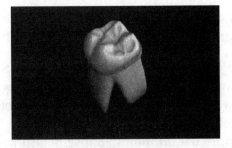

The Virtual Tooth can be rotated if you have the Apple Quick-Time plug-in installed with your browser. Students can use the mouse to rotate the tooth and look at all the sides.

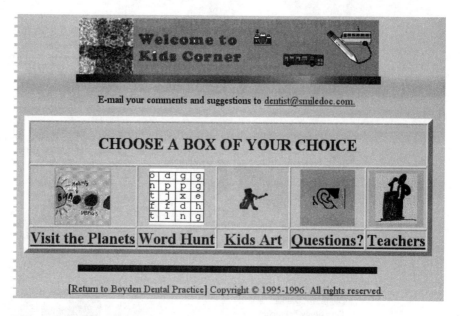

There is also a Kids Corner with puzzles and games they can play
while learning about teeth. The dentists have also provided answers
to commonly asked questions about teeth and visits to the dentist.

Other Teeth and Nutrition Websites:

So You Want to Be a Dentist?
(different kinds of dentists, how to become a dentist, images of
dental procedures)
http://www.vvm.com/~bond/home.htm

The Tooth Fairy
(1st graders stories & pictures about the Tooth Fairy)
http://www.clark.net/pub/cve/teeth.html

The Tooth Fairy—Marc Grossman DDS
(information about a dentist's office, dental first aid, and a dialog
between Lizzie Lion & Freddie Frog about what to do if a tooth is
knocked out)
http://www.infopoint.com/sc/health/pediatric-dentistry/

Apple QuickTime Virtual Reality plug-in (QTVR)
http://www.apple.com/quicktime/

THE BRAIN AND NERVOUS SYSTEM

Neuroscience for Kids

These pages will be a valuable resource for you and your students after you download them and store them on your computer. There is a wealth of information about the brain and nervous system as well as lesson ideas, clear and descriptive graphics, and even sound files to help you learn how to pronounce many scientific terms.

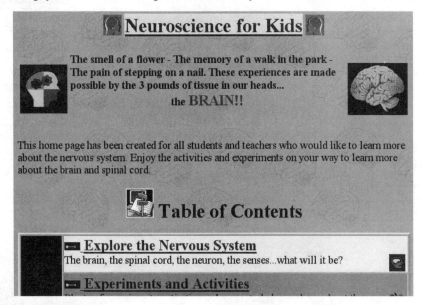

Neuroscience for Kids
Used with the permission of Dr. Eric H. Chudler
http://Weber.u.washington.edu/~chudler/neurok.html

You could use *Web Buddy*'s Site To Go utility to download all or part of this Web site.

Have students look for diagrams of various parts of the nervous system and draw their own diagrams. Once you have completed your study of the nervous system, you could even send the drawings or scanned images to Dr. Chudler for him to include on his Web site.

The Web site contains detailed reference information about each part of the nervous system as well as classroom activities and experiments.

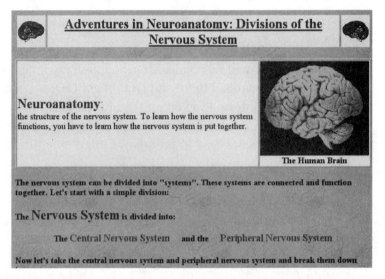

 Dr. Chudler has recorded sound files for many of those hard-to-pronounce scientific terms. Once you have used the Site To Go utility to download all the files and you have saved the Web pages to your hard drive, the sound files will play almost immediately when you click on the hypertext links.

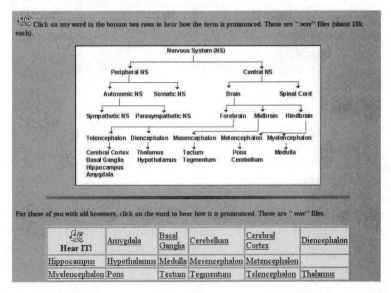

In the Brain Worksheets and Puzzles section, you will find a reproducible scavenger hunt worksheet designed just for this Web site. You can print it as is or you can use *Web Buddy*'s Convert utility to convert it into a document for your word processor.

There are printable diagrams for students to color and label. There are also word search puzzles and crossword puzzles with hints. You can even find instructions for making brain models.

Comparative Mammalian Brain Collections

If you are looking for printable photos of various brains, you can find them at this Web site from the University of Wisconsin and Michigan State University.

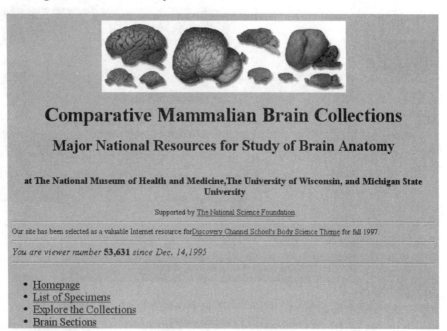

Comparative Mammalian Brain Collections

Major National Resources for Study of Brain Anatomy

at The National Museum of Health and Medicine, The University of Wisconsin, and Michigan State University

Supported by The National Science Foundation

Our site has been selected as a valuable Internet resource for Discovery Channel School's Body Science Theme for fall 1997.

You are viewer number **53,631** *since Dec. 14, 1995*

- Homepage
- List of Specimens
- Explore the Collections
- Brain Sections

Comparative Mammalian Brain Collections
http://www.neurophys.wisc.edu/brain/

You could assign students a particular mammal to study having them find photographs of the brains at these Web sites. Once you have used Site To Go to download these pages, the graphics will appear much more quickly.

The Human Body

Students could create Web pages about parts of the nervous system or parts of the body. You can incorporate them into a "Web site" to keep on your computer or to upload to an online location.

Sixth graders in Mrs. Sutton's class at Fair Oaks Elementary School in Oakdale, California, made Web pages with short reports, recorded sound files, and scanned drawings to tell about the parts of the body.

You could use the Site To Go utility to download the reports or just use Page To Go and then look at the HTML coding in your browser's editor. This is a very simple way for your students and you to see how a Web page is created.

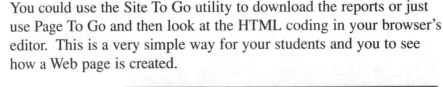

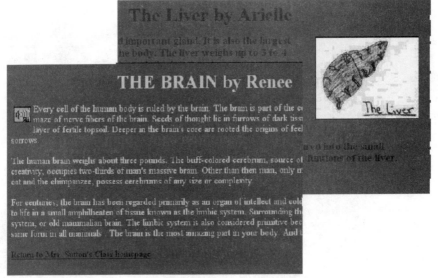

Mrs. Sutton's Class—The Human Body Website
http://www.eusd.stan-co.k12.ca.us/stroud/sutton/index.html

They could also create a multimedia presentation using software such as *HyperStudio* to share with other classes. This would also be a wonderful presentation for a parents' night at school It's a great way to illustrate how you are using the technology in your school and classroom.

The Brain is the Boss

The My Body Web site is a wonderful teaching tool. The graphics are clear and this would be a good addition to a center with models of basic body parts for the students to study while browsing this site offline once you have downloaded it with the Site To Go utility.

The Brain is the Boss

Meet the Brain - The Boss of Your Body

How do you remember the way to your friend's house? Why do your eyes blink without you ever thinking about it? Where do dreams come from? Your brain is the one responsible for these things, and a whole lot more. Your brain is the boss of your body. It runs the show by controlling just about everything you do.

- It is more powerful and much faster than any computer you've ever used.
- It is large and in charge - so large that it fills the upper half of your head.
- It looks like a soft, wrinkly gray sponge, and it's almost as heavy as a carton of orange juice! By the time you're grown up, it will weigh about three pounds.

Your brain is made up of several parts, and it's time to introduce them. Let's give a warm KidsHealth welcome to . . .

The Brain is the Boss
(part of My Body by KidsHealth.org (c) The Nemours Foundation)
http://kidshealth.org/kid/somebody/index.html

The Brain Model Tutorial

This site, created by Mark Darty and Dr. James Brody, is a tutorial of all the parts of the brain. From glands to cerebellum, there are illustrations and information which would make a good resource for your classroom.

Where the My Body Web site might be for younger students, the information at this tutorial is geared more toward older students and teachers.

Psychology Electronic Teaching Source
http://pegasus.cc.ucf.edu/~Brainmd1/index.html

At this index page, you will find the link for the Brain Model Tutorial. You will also find materials online (brain images and graphics) that are in the public domain (MRI imaging, photo of human brain, diagrams).

Brain Model Tutorial
http://pegasus.cc.ucf.edu/~Brainmd1/brain2.html

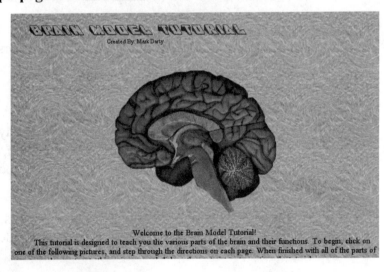

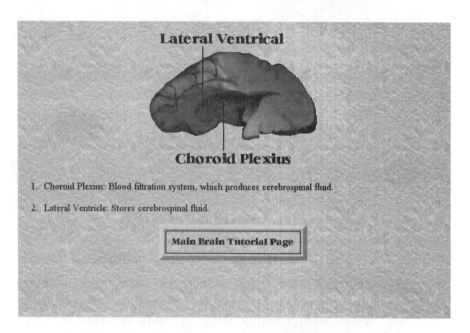

Lateral Ventrical

Choroid Plexius

1. Choroid Plexius: Blood filtration system, which produces cerebrospinal fluid.

2. Lateral Ventricle: Stores cerebrospinal fluid.

Main Brain Tutorial Page

The parts of the brain are separated and clearly identified. This would be a good teaching tool if you downloaded it using the Site To Go utility. Then it could be used on a large screen for the whole class to see, or used as a small group activity at one computer.

Other Brain and Nervous System Web Sites:

The Dana Foundation—sponsors of Brain Awareness Week
http://www.dana.org/brainweek

Images of the Drosophila Nervous System
(contains a clickable brain diagram with explanations of parts—being incorporated into Flybrain site listed below)
http://brain.biologie.uni-freiburg.de/Atlas/text/atlasFi.html

Flybrain—An Online Atlas and Database of the Drosophila Nervous System
http://www.flybrain.org

BioBook—Nervous System
Estrella Mountain Community College
http://www.emc.maricopa.edu/bio/bio181/BIOBK/BioBookNERV.html

TOUR A DINOSAUR MUSEUM

Ever wanted to take your students on a tour of a museum and couldn't raise the money or get permission or find the time or...? Well, here are some opportunities to take your students on a tour of dinosaur exhibits.

Many natural history museums are placing electronic virtual tours of their exhibits online. They include photographs of the exhibits, text descriptions of what is in the photographs as well as audio files of a museum docent explaining the exhibit.

Honolulu Community College Dinosaur Exhibit

In Hawaii, there is a permanent exhibit of dinosaur fossils for free public viewing. The "fossils" are replicas from originals at the American Museum of Natural History in New York City.

Honolulu Community College

Dinosaurs in Hawaii!

Honolulu Community College invites you...

For the first time in Hawaii, there is a unique, free, **permanent** exhibit of dinosaur fossils available for public viewing. These "fossils" are replicas from the originals at the American Museum of Natural History in New York City, which boasts one of the finest and largest collections of dinosaur fossils in the world.

HCC is providing Hawaii's students and interested community groups with an exciting look at the prehistoric natural history of the world by displaying the fossils of some of the largest terrestrial creatures that ever lived. Knowledgeable docents can give presentations geared to different age levels.

Honolulu Community College Dinosaur Exhibit
http://www.hcc.hawaii.edu/dinos/dinos.1.html

This online exhibit of the collection of fossils has audio files of Rick Ziegler, one of the exhibit's founders, narrating the tour. Students simply click on the speaker icon to hear the recording as they read along.

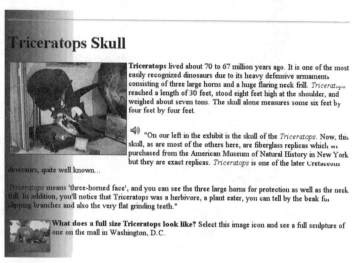

By using the Site To Go utility, you can download this tour and have your students visit the dinosaur exhibits right at your computer. They will see Triceratops, Tyrannosaurus, Stegosaurus, Hypselosaurus, Iguanadon, and Deinonychus exhibits. Some of these are fossil reproductions and others are sculptures. If you click on the small photographs at the exhibits, you will see a larger photograph. There are also movie files at some of the exhibits. They are in .mpeg format and will play if you have that type of movie player on your computer.

Let your students work in pairs or teams at your computer to take a tour of this virtual museum. You could post a series of questions beside your computer and have the students visit the museum in order to find the answers.

Students can use these exhibits as guidelines for creating a multimedia project of their own classroom virtual zoo. By visiting other dinosaur exhibits, students can gather information, photographs, or graphics and create their own *HyperStudio* or Web page project.

Dinosaurs: Facts and Fiction

USGS
science for a changing world

Dinosaurs:
Facts and Fiction

By Ronald J. Litwin, Robert E. Weems, and Thomas R. Holtz, Jr.

Few subjects in the Earth sciences are as fascinating to the public as dinosaurs. The study of dinosaurs stretches our imaginations, gives us new perspectives on time and space, and invites us to discover worlds very different from our modern Earth.

From a scientific viewpoint, however, the study of dinosaurs is important both for understanding the causes of past major extinctions of land animals and for understanding the changes in biological diversity caused by previous geological and climatic changes of the Earth. These changes are still occurring today. A wealth of new information about dinosaurs has been learned over the past 30 years, and science's old ideas of dinosaurs as slow, clumsy beasts have been totally turned around. This pamphlet contains answers to some frequently

Dinosaurs: Facts and Fiction
http://pubs.usgs.gov/gip/dinosaurs/

Created by the USGS (U.S. Geological Survey), this Web site has a series of articles with scientific information about dinosaurs. Each article answers a questions such as these:

> When did the first dinosaurs appear on Earth?
>
> Are all fossil animals dinosaurs?
>
> Did people and dinosaurs live at the same time?
>
> Where did dinosaurs live?
>
> Did all the dinosaurs live together, and at the same time?
>
> How are dinosaurs named?

There are many more questions answered. You and your students may enjoy reading through this information on your search for material for developing that virtual dinosaur museum. Use the Site To Go utility to download this set of pages.

Students can create posters about different types of dinosaurs from the information they find in the Web sites you download. The poster could include pictures and/or a short report about the dinosaur.

You might have them make trading cards for a dinosaur like those associated with comic book super-heroes or athletes. Use several baseball or football cards as examples and have students find a picture for the front of their card with the dinosaur's name. Then put particular data on the back of the card, such as full scientific name, size, type of food it ate, and location.

Copy the cards so that each student has enough copies of his or her card to trade with the entire class as well as extras for friends who aren't in the same classroom. Then schedule a card-trading day. Copy the cards on cardstock paper (front and back) and have the students cut them out ahead of time.

If you don't have the technology for your students to create a "virtual museum," they can create dioramas or picture museums on posterboard by using pictures and photographs they have printed from the Web pages you have downloaded.

Other Dinosaur Web Sites:

American Museum of Natural History
(home of the original fossils in the Honolulu museum)
http://www.amnh.org/

Dinosaur Headlines—E-news
(information about current scientific discoveries about dinosaurs)
http://www.amnh.org/enews/dinohead.html

Monroe Middle School—Green River, WY
http://monhome.sw2.k12.wy.us/

A Tour of Dinosaur National Monument—Discovering Dinosaurs
(a student project about the National Monument—great example)
http://monhome.sw2.k12.wy.us/Dinos/intro.html

Smithsonian Institution Natural History Web Home Page
http://www.mnh.si.edu/nmnhweb.html

The NMNH Virtual Tour
(includes dinosaur exhibits on the First Floor)
http://www.nmnh.si.edu/VirtualTour/index.html

Royal Tyrrell Museum
http://tyrrell.magtech.ab.ca/home.html

Dinosaur Hall
http://tyrrell.magtech.ab.ca/tour/dinohall.html

Field Museum of Natural History—Chicago
http://www.fmnh.org./

Online Exhibits with teachers guide to the exhibit
http://www.fmnh.org./exhibits/Web_exhibits.htm

Dinosauria On-Line
(includes an omnipedia with dinosaur information and a picture
gallery you might download for graphics for your student projects)
http://www.dinosauria.com/

The Natural History Museum—London
http://www.nhm.ac.uk/index.html

Dinosaur data files
(This museum has dinosaur data cards for 28 different dinosaurs with
specific information about each one—similar to trading cards. They
can be printed and then copied on hard stock paper and used as
teaching tools. There is also an Excel spreadsheet with the data from
the cards which can be downloaded.)
http://www.nhm.ac.uk/education/activity/dinosaurs/

The Dinosauria
http://www.ucmp.berkeley.edu/diapsids/dinosaur.html

The Dinosaur Art Gallery of Joe Tucciarone
http://members.aol.com/Dinoplanet/dinosaur.html

Dinosaur Resources on the Web
(additional links which may take you to even more virtual museums)
**http://www.service.emory.edu/GEOSCIENCE/HTML/DinoLinks.
htm**

TAKE FLIGHT

There are many resources available online for you to use while teaching your students about airplanes and flight. Some tell the history of flight while others offer you detailed plans for having your students create different types of model flying machines for classroom test flights.

Off to a Flying Start

This is a learning project aimed at students in grades K–2. It teaches about how airplanes fly through the use of diagrams and models.

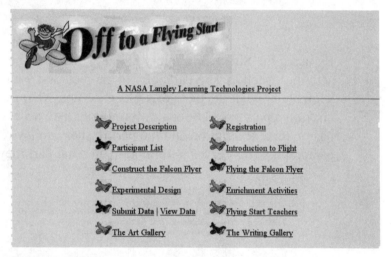

Off to a Flying Start
http://k12unix.larc.nasa.gov/flyingstart/

This was designed to be an online project with different classes participating at the same time and comparing data as they do some of the activities. There are also quite a lot of activities you can do with your students, even if you're not participating with the group.

Please be sure to let them know you're working with the program, though. The more online projects like this are utilized, the more they're likely to be able to fund and provide.

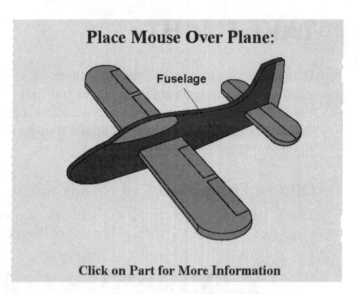

Place Mouse Over Plane:

Fuselage

Click on Part for More Information

 By using the Site To Go utility and downloading the online tutorial activities, such as The Parts of a Plane, you and your students can learn about what the parts of a plane are and what they do. If they click on a part for additional information, they access another Web page with a description and the part flashes as they read the paragraph. This serves to remind them what part they chose.

Procedure

1. Print the template and cut out the wing, fuselage, and elevator.
2. Trace the wing, fueslage, and elevator templates on the styrofoam tray. Cut out the stryofoam wings, fuselage, and elevator with a plastic knife or scissors. (I found the scissors to be the easiest to use with the styrofoam.) Cut the elevator and wing slots on the fuselage.

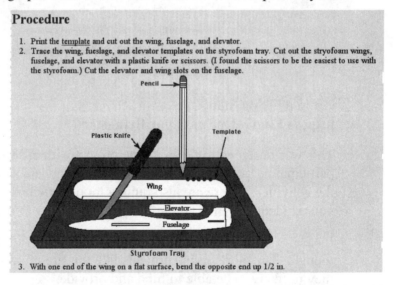

Pencil

Plastic Knife   Template

Wing

Elevator

Fuselage

Styrofoam Tray

3. With one end of the wing on a flat surface, bend the opposite end up 1/2 in.

There is also a set of plans for making an airplane, The Falcon Flyer, out of styrofoam meat trays.

Exploring With Aviation Education

These activities are sponsored by the Minnesota Department of Transportation, Office of Aeronautics. The Web site is maintained by Kelly Jahn (kelly.jahn@aero.dot.state.mn.us). There are many activities here for students of all ages.

Exploring with Aviation Education
http://www.dot.state.mn.us/aeronautics/AVEDU/mdotedu.html

Wendy Altobell's Flight Unit

Wendy's unit, aimed at 1st graders, teaches them the parts of an airplane and how they work. It is designed to be used during a 3-week unit.

The parts of the unit include:

> Lesson 1: Constructing and Flying the Ring Wing Plane
> Lesson 2: Constructing and Experimenting with the Gyrocopter
> Lesson 3: Constructing and Flying the Boomerang
> Lesson 4: Constructing and Flying the Foam Glider
> Lesson 5: Experimenting with Balloon Rockets
> Lesson 6: Hot Air Balloon Launch

1. Fold typing or similar size/weight paper diagonally so that the corners do not meet.

2. Make two or more folds on front, each about one half inch wide.

3. With the fold on the inside, form the paper into a circle. Slip one pointy end into the other.

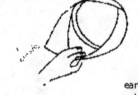

4. To fly the ring wing hold with two fingers on top of the 'vee', the thumb on the bottom, and toss with a sm-o-o-o-th follow through. Too much speed or the lack of a follow through are no no's.

early French Ring Wing design

Wendy Altobell Flight Unit
**http://www.dot.state.mn.us/aeronautics/AVEDU/CURRICULA/A
LTOBELL/waflight_unit.html**

There are directions for making several different styles of paper airplane models that fly. You can use the Site To Go utility to download all the plans in order to have them available for the students to print. (Remember to make your own models first as guidelines for the students.)

Darla Olson's Aerospace Unit

This is a Kindergarten unit which could be used as part of a unit about transportation. It teaches about how airplanes work and has activities about gliders, hot air balloons, helicopters, and space travel.

The students learn about the external airplane parts and the altimeter, air speed indicator, tachometer, and compass. There are instructions for making a "pre-kite" from a paper bag and string. There is another design for a styrofoam glider. You could have teams make both types of gliders, schedule test flights for both gliders, then compare the results. (Ask your local supermarket if they would donate "unused" styrofoam trays for your activity.)

Landing Gear

The wheels and the parts that attach the wheels to the fuselage make up the landing gear. The landing gear is also used to taxi, takeoff and land. The landing gear isn't needed in the air for flying. Therefor, during flight large airplanes fold (retract) the landing gear into the fuselage or wing. This makes the airplane aerodynamic (sleek in shape). Small airplanes do not have landing gear that folds up.

Landing Gear

Diagram of plane part—Darla Olson's Aerospace Unit
**http://www.dot.state.mn.us/aeronautics/AVEDU/CURRICULA/O
LSON/do_aero.html**

The diagram Web page could be converted or translated to a document for a word processor. Then enlarge the type and post each part and its description on a bulletin board display along with photographs of airplanes from magazines. You could also print them on overhead transparency film with an inkjet or deskjet printer for use while you are teaching the class. (Remember to use only inkjet or deskjet transparency film and to set your printer to print transparency quality.)

Aviation and Space Curriculum Guide

Designed for students in grades K–3, this unit has lessons and activities for these topics:

> History of Aerospace
> Kinds and Uses of Aircraft
> Parts of an Airplane
> Why Aircraft Fly
> Weather
> Instruments and Navigation
> Airports

There are complete instructions for many activities in each topic. There are also ready-to-use handouts that you can download using the Page To Go utility, if you don't need the entire Web site.

STUDENT HANDOUT 9

Directions: Read each airplane description. Cut and paste next to the correct airplane.

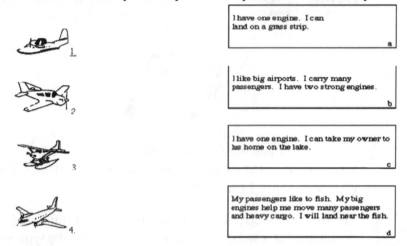

1.

2.

3.

4.

> I have one engine. I can land on a grass strip.
>
> a

> I like big airports. I carry many passengers. I have two strong engines.
>
> b

> I have one engine. I can take my owner to his home on the lake.
>
> c

> My passengers like to fish. My big engines help me move many passengers and heavy cargo. I will land near the fish.
>
> d

Aviation & Space Curriculum Guide K-3
**http://www.dot.state.mn.us/aeronautics/AVEDU/CURRICULA/E
DK-3/edk-3.html**

This is a sample activity that you could convert to a word processing file and then print as a worksheet for your students to complete. They must cut out the descriptions and paste them next to the correct airplanes. This is just one example of many activities you will find in this unit plan.

Future Aspiring Aviators

For those students interested in learning to fly or work with airplanes, this unit covers many of the important issues they need to learn about. It is designed for students in grades K–3 and covers topics such as weather, gravity, air, and aircraft.

You may want to Convert the worksheet pages of this unit into word processing files for printing purposes. This is a good way to have a document that you can use just part of at one time. You can adjust the instructions for the age of your students. You could also make the font size larger for younger students.

This site also has a study photo section which has photographs and descriptions of a bi-plane, jet plane, helicopter, and passenger plane. You could convert these to word processing files and enlarge the font size or print on transparency film to use with the whole class.

Helicopter

Helicopters do not have wings like most other airplanes. They have rotating blades above the body of the plane. The blades provide for lift, propulsion and steering of the helicopter. Helicopters can take off vertically rising right straight up in the air. They can hover (remain in one spot in the air) and fly in any direction. Helicopters have a tail rotor (like a small propeller in a more vertical position) to prevent the helicopter body from spinning around and around.

Future Aspiring Aviators

http://www.dot.state.mn.us/aeronautics/AVEDU/CURRICULA/ K-3/k3.html

You could also include this information if you do the transportation lesson in this book, "How We Get Around." Your students could use these photographs and information when they create their time lines of the history of transportation.

Reading & Activity Publications

Another section in this Web site has various publications you can download and use with your students. There are 4 units of online books called "The Sky's The Limit." They cover the following topics:

> Early Days of Flight
> Pilots Help Our Nation
> A Place in the Sky
> Beyond the Earth

Not all of the subjects of the books are famous pilots, but they are all people who have made valuable contributions to the field of aviation.

There are activities and worksheets to accompany each of the stories.

Charles Lindbergh

Charles Lindbergh was born in Detroit, Michigan on February 4, 1902. When he was very young, his family moved to a farm in central Minnesota near a town called Little Falls. His father was a United States congressman and his mother taught chemistry at the high school. Charles liked living the outdoor life in Minnesota. He helped with the farming and enjoyed swimming in the Mississippi river. Whenever his father was home from Washington D.C., he and Charles would go hunting. Young Charles was fascinated by the sight of airplanes. They were a new invention then and a thrill to see.

The Sky's the Limit—Charles Lindbergh
**http://www.dot.state.mn.us/aeronautics/AVEDU/PUBLICATIONS/
publications.html**

The subjects of the books are:

Charles Lindbergh
Amelia Earhart
Benjamin Davis, Jr.
Elizabeth Wall Strohfus
Jeana Yeager
Anne Morrow Lindbergh
Mary Ross
Franklin Chang—Diaz

Bessie Coleman
Angelo De Ponti
Phoebe Fairgrave Omlie
Bennie L. Davis
Randy Penner
Mark Hurd
Paul Pao

You might download all four parts of the series by using the Site To Go utility. Then have pairs of students read about different subjects and present their information to the rest of the class.

Other Aerospace Web Sites:

Mark Powell's Hot Air Balloon and Other Links
http://Web2.airmail.net/markpowl/balloon.html

National Air & Space Museum
http://www.nasm.edu/

Paper Airplanes on the Internet (instructions for folding)
http://pchelp.inc.net/paper_ac.htm

Virtual Tour of Boeing 727 Cockpit (photo images and description of what is in the photos)
http://www.net-works.net/community/msd/727index.htm

Delta Planes
http://www.delta-air.com/trip_a2z/planes/planes.htm

Southwest Airlines Photo Gallery
(cockpit of a Boeing 737, jets taking off, on the ground, on flight deck of an aircraft carrier, and past advertisement video clips)
http://www.iflyswa.com/info/photos.html

Boeing Company
(photo gallery, virtual tours, digital videos, and a screensaver)
http://www.boeing.com/

Illustrated History of Boeing, aircraft from the bi-planes to the Space Shuttle
http://www.boeing.com/companyoffices/history/

TWA—airplane photographs and seating maps
http://www.twa.com

Lesson Plan about *The Wright Brothers,* book by Russell Freedman
http://www.umcs.maine.edu/~orono/collaborative/wright.html

The K-8 Aeronautics Internet Textbook
http://wings.ucdavis.edu/

PREPARE FOR LIFT-OFF

Exploring the universe is the subject of movies and television programs and is certainly in the minds of children. Whether out of simple curiosity or a desire to join the space program, students will enjoy learning about the Space Shuttle, its astronauts, and its many missions.

Clickable Space Shuttle

A wonderful teaching tool can be found at this Web site. Part of the Student Space Awareness Virtual Headquarters, the Clickable Space Shuttle is an illustrated guide to all the parts of a shuttle.

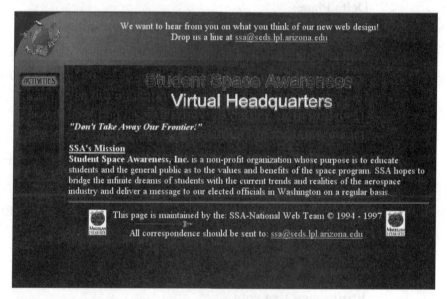

Student Space Awareness Virtual Headquarters
http://seds.lpl.arizona.edu/ssa/index2.html

You can download it with the Site To Go utility and have access to information about the shuttle ready at your computer the next time there is a launch. Although the text is for older students, the younger children will enjoy clicking on the parts of the shuttle and seeing larger graphics while you explain to them what the parts do.

Clickable Space Shuttle
http://seds.lpl.arizona.edu/ssa/docs/Space.Shuttle/index.shtml

© Student Space Awareness and Joshua S. Mussaf
http://www.seds.org/ssa/

Create a center activity with questions posted at the computer about the various parts of the shuttle. Have students rotate through the center in teams trying to find the answers.

The NASA Shuttle Web

NASA (National Aeronautics & Space Administration) has several Web sites online at different locations throughout the country. Each Web site concentrates on activities at that space center.

The Shuttle Web site provides information about shuttle missions. It keeps an archive of past launch information and continually updates current missions. It even announces future missions in advance so that you can start planning your lessons.

There is information about launch schedules, delays, mission objectives, astronaut biographical information, and a link to the Space Team Online Web site which has project ideas for your students.

Sneak Preview

Previous Missions * * * Future Missions * * * Internatioɩ

January 22 is the launch date for the first flight of 1998 and the eighth to rendezvous and dock with Russia's Mir Ɔpaⅽ. Statioɩ.

This flight of Endeavour is the eighth in a series of nⅈⅆ planned shuttle missions to rendezvous with, and dock to, tⅈⅆ space station Mir, restocking the Russian outpost with suppⅼⅇ; and transferring American crewmembers, while conductⅈⅆₓ on-orbit science and continuing a series of tests designed tⅈ prove concepts the two countries will employ when they begⅈ. assembling the International Space Station later thⅈₐ yⅈₐₐ

For two of the astronauts this is a return trip to Mⅈ.

Endeavour on
Launch Pad A

The NASA Shuttle Web
http://shuttle.nasa.gov/index.html/

During a shuttle mission, schedule *Web Buddy* to download the daily mission updates so that you would have them ready to take to school each day.

Kennedy Space Center

Another NASA Web site, this site contains current data about missions, image archives, movie files, photographs of rockets, shuttles, and satellites, as well as photographs of Earth taken from space. It is another source of archived shuttle mission information and information about the astronauts.

If your classroom computer is online, you might want to view the live video feeds from the Kennedy Space Center. They are set to "refresh" every 90 seconds but you can reduce the delay using the Control Panel on the Web page. There is a weather monitoring screen, a NASA-TV view, a view of the Vehicle Assembly Building, the Space Station Processing Facility, and the Launch Pad. You can click on these graphics to get a larger photograph.

Kennedy Space Center Home Page
http://www.ksc.nasa.gov/

NASA - KSC Video Feeds

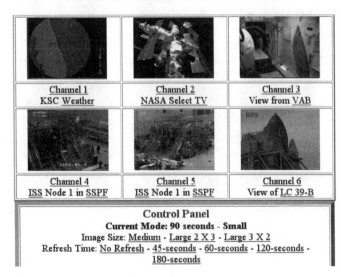

Kennedy Space Center Live Video Feeds
http://www.ksc.nasa.gov/shuttle/countdown/video/video.html

Once your students have browsed through all your collected Web sites, you could have them create posters to promote support for the space program or travel brochures for a future shuttle launch using the photographs found in those sites or others you may download.

Other Space Shuttle Web Sites:

Space Shuttle Photographs
http://ceps.nasm.edu:2020/RPIF/SSPR.html

NASA/Marshall Space Flight Center
http://www.msfc.nasa.gov/

The Astronaut Connection
http://nauts.com/

NASA—JSC Digital Image Collection (photograph archive)
http://images.jsc.nasa.gov/

Educational Space Simulations Project
http://chico.rice.edu/armadillo/Simulations/simserver.html

HoustonChronicle.com Space Central
http://www.chron.com/content/interactive/space/index.html

LIFE ON OTHER PLANETS?

Do your students think there might be life on other planets or their moons? This would be a great way to have them use current information to provide them with data to draw scientific conclusions of their own.

Several sites online have graphics and data about each of the planets and their moons.

The Nine Planets

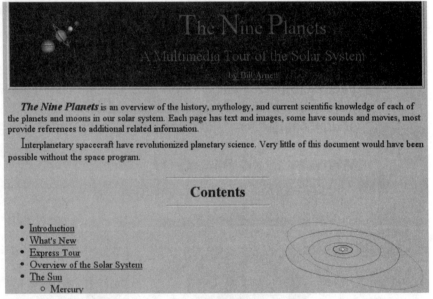

The Nine Planets is an overview of the history, mythology, and current scientific knowledge of each of the planets and moons in our solar system. Each page has text and images, some have sounds and movies, most provide references to additional related information.

Interplanetary spacecraft have revolutionized planetary science. Very little of this document would have been possible without the space program.

Contents

* Introduction
* What's New
* Express Tour
* Overview of the Solar System
* The Sun
  * Mercury

The Nine Planets
http://seds.lpl.arizona.edu/nineplanets/nineplanets/nineplanets.html

This Web site has photographs and information about all the planets as well as each of their moons. There is also information about other small bodies such as comets, asteroids and meteors.

Use *Web Buddy*'s Site To Go utility to download this site. Be aware that some of the links go outside this Web site, but you should be able to obtain the basic graphics and the data posted there.

Each page about a planet or orbiting satellite body contains information about it such as diameter, distance from the sun, length of orbit, atmosphere, and composition of the crust.

Welcome to the Planets

Welcome to the Planets
http://pds.jpl.nasa.gov/planets/

Welcome to the Planets is another source of current planetary data online.

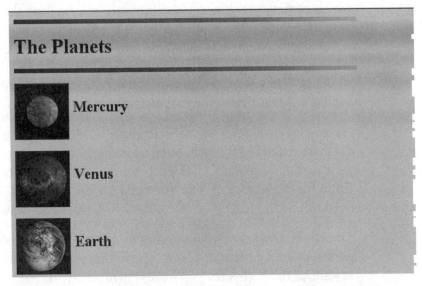

It is similar to The Nine Planets and has data about each of the planets in a section of each page called Planet Profile. Your students should find atmospheric and crust composition data.

Have your students use the Web pages to find information about the possibility of life being or ever being on their selected planet.

They should pay attention to the following data:

> Type of atmosphere/air—chemical composition
> Temperature—highs and lows in comparison to that of Earth
> Daylight—would there be enough sunlight to support plant growth
> Evidence of water—living things, as we know them, must have a source of water

Once they have reached a team conclusion, they could print some of the photos of their planet and make a poster to support their view.

They could use desktop publishing software to create a travel brochure for their planet, including data to convince people that it would support life.

Once you have several different resources available, you might also want to have your students make a comparison chart of certain pieces of data and research the different information they find. Be sure to include some older reference books so that they can see the difference between data available 5 and 10 (or more) years ago and what we know today. Discuss the reliability of data with your students. They should learn to look for the most current data available when researching scientific questions.

Have several students create a database of planetary data. Have the database available for each team of students to enter the data for their particular planet. Give each team a worksheet with blanks to fill in for each piece of data you need for the database. They may need to look at more than one source to find all the answers.

You could divide your class into 9 teams and students could create a poster about a particular planet. Have them include data from several of the Web sites you have downloaded. These sites also have superb photographs of the planets that they could print and use on their posters. Each team could be that planet's expert scientists and they could research questions posed by other teams' members and report back to the class daily.

Other Solar System Web sites:

Views of the Solar System
http://www.hawastsoc.org/solar/homepage.htm

USGS, Flagstaff Solar System Images
http://wwwflag.wr.usgs.gov/USGSFlag/Images/images.html

Planet and Space Mission Information—NASA
http://www.nasa.gov/

StarChild—The Solar System—NASA
http://starchild.gsfc.nasa.gov/docs/StarChild/solar_system_level1/ solar_system.html

Our Solar System of Planets
http://www.ici.net/cust_pages/automan/astronomy/pg000005.htm

MEXICAN ART

Diego Rivera Virtual Museum

Diego Rivera was a muralist painter from Mexico. This Web site has digital images of some of his work as well as historical information about the artist's life in both English and Spanish.

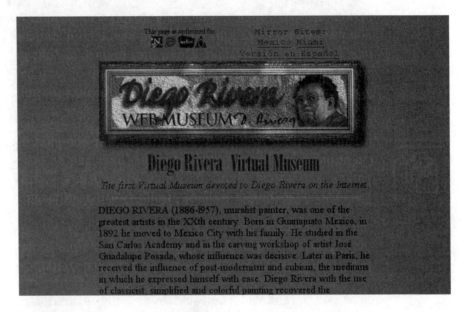

Diego Rivera Virtual Museum
http://www.diegorivera.com/diego_home_eng.html

This would be a valuable resource in Art and Spanish Language classes as well as in regular classrooms. It has a large quantity of graphics and is a good example of a Site To Go that should be downloaded at a later time rather than while you are sitting in front of your computer watching it.

The online gallery houses digital images of paintings and murals located in various collections. You may only want to choose several paintings or murals to study in your class. Many of them depict scenes through history or life in Mexican cities.

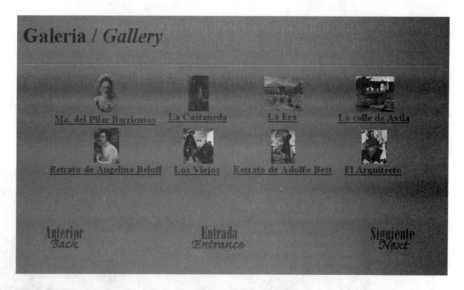

The Gallery has small, or thumbnail, digital images of the paintings and murals. If you click on the thumbnails, you will see a larger version of each item. You can use *Web Buddy*'s Page To Go utility to download several pages.

You can choose the ones you want to download and then set *Web Buddy*'s Scheduling utility to download them all at one time later in the day.

Once you have downloaded several paintings or murals, have your students work in teams to analyze them. You may choose topics as simple as color and perspective or more in-depth concepts as style, realism, content, or historical background.

You can create a mural of your own about a location or historical event in Mexico's history. Use large roll paper for a giant mural or use connected computer paper for a smaller one. Different teams of students could design different murals and finish them in different media: mosaic, paint, chalk, or colored pencil.

Welcome to The Masks of God

Welcome to The Masks of God

W elcome to the Huichol Art Gallery known as **The Masks of God**.

The Masks of God—Art of the Huichol
http://www.themasksofgod.com/

This Web site shows the Masks and other art pieces of the Huichol artisans. The history of the beadwork and explanations of the symbols are also explained. An important part of this Web page is the philosophy that this true artistry be preserved and not exploited through poor quality mass reproduction.

 You can use *Web Buddy*'s Site To Go option to download several or all of these pages. There are enlarged graphics which you can access by clicking on the thumbnail versions.

Your students could choose their favorite design and recreate it in a different art form, such as mosaic or in paints. You could provide older students with small beads and have them design pieces of art on a smaller scale, such as the egg designs shown at this site or as small ornaments.

By creating even a small piece of representative artwork, your students will gain a respect for the talent and patience of the Huichol artisans. They will learn about the culture of this region of Mexico.

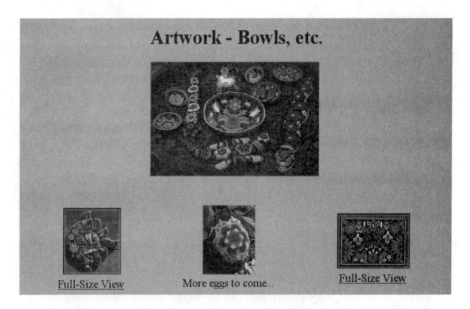

They could use the many examples shown at this Web site as ideas for their own designs.

Other Huichol(e) Art Web Sites:

Huichol Indians—their Art and Symbols
http://www.hypermex.com/html/abt_huit.htm

Huichole Art (bead work and yarn paintings)
http://www.zapcom.net/phoenix.arabeth/Huichol.html

Other Mexican Art Web Sites:

Frida Kahlo's Art
http://www.cascade.net/kahlo.html

University of Guadalajara Website with Art Galleries
http://udgftp.cencar.udg.mx/ingles/CUAAD-INGLES.html

Background About the Art of Mexico
http://www.travelleader.com/tlpr/mexico/mexic8.htm

Mini-Unit about Mexico
http://multimedia2.freac.fsu.edu/academy/k1mexico.htm

THE MAGIC OF MUSIC

Music World for Kids

Rhythm, pitch, meter—what do those have to do with computers? Music World's Web site has lessons, complete with representative sound files, for teaching those concepts and more.

MUSIC WORLD
FOR KIDS

welcome to **Music World For Kids**. Music World is an instructional aid to basic music education. Each page focuses on a different topic, giving you information on music basics along with exercises to help improve your skills. Listening buttons are scattered throughout to make learning more fun.(All sound bytes are in "*.wav" format and should be listened to using a PC wave player like Sound Recorder in MS-Windows.)

Music World for Kids
http://members.aol.com/muswrld/

Sheri Zalar has created this Web site as a resource for music educators. There are graphics of musical notation, treble and bass clef notes and their corresponding piano keys, and examples of common types of meters. By using Site To Go, you could have this on your computer in your classroom or music room as a teaching tool or as a review.

Students could work in groups at the computer as they read through the different lessons and play the sound files. They could clap along as they replay the rhythm sounds. Have students practice finding the keys on a keyboard or practice sheet as they read through the musical notation exercises.

RHYTHM

BEAT Beats are regular pulses that are the basis for measuring time in music. The unit is not a minute or second but rather a unit of time established by the musician who chooses the speed of the music

* Pick hear to DOWNLOAD and listen to a beat

TEMPO The speed of the music varies from one piece of music to another. Tempo is the term we use for describing the speed of the music. Common terms used to refer to tempo are

Slow Tempo _____ Fast Tempo

Largo Lento Adagio Andante Allegro Presto

* Pick hear to DOWNLOAD and listen to a Lento tempo

* Pick hear to DOWNLOAD and listen to a Allegro tempo

SIMPLE DIVISION OF THE BEAT Simple division of the beat is when the beat is divided into two equal parts. For example, if the beat is assigned the half note, then the division of the beat will be indicated by quarter notes.

You could use this Web site as an example for students to create Web pages of their own. They could work in teams to record simple rhythms and then describe them on the Web page in words or graphics. If you have them write rhythms or melodies and harmonies on staff paper, you could scan those in and incorporate into the Web page along with the sound file.

Music, The Universal Language

This is another Web site created with teachers in mind by music educator Deborah Jeter. She created this Web site and is a columnist at Suite 101—Music Education, as well.

There are links to music software and artists' Web pages but the best pages are the Fun Music Ideas sent in by readers of the Web site—music and classroom teachers like you—and the Seasonal Activities.

The Seasonal Activities include rhythm practices and old songs with new lyrics along with a storehouse of musical graphics for use with Web pages or multimedia presentations.

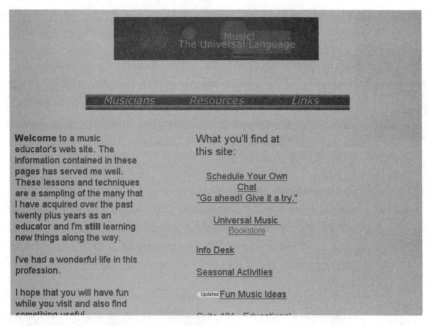

Music, The Universal Language
http://www.jumpoint.com/bluesman/

If you would like to submit a lesson idea for her next newsletter, please e-mail her at bluesman1@earthlink.net.

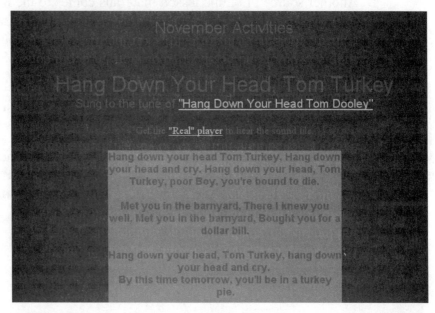

The "Tom Turkey" song is one of the Seasonal Activities at her Web site. Making up new lyrics for songs can be a fun project for you and your students.

 The special November song of "Hang Down Your Head, Tom Turkey" has a Real Audio file which will download with the Site To Go utility if you set it to download that page and go one level deep. It will play from your local disk drive then if you have a Real Audio player and sound card.

Your students could create an even bigger project by finding the midi sound files for the songs and creating a group of Web pages with the new lyrics and the playable sound files to have at your fingertips. If you have Real Player Plus, you could also record students singing or playing various songs and incorporate those recordings into the Web pages.

 The Web site also has a music images gallery full of graphics which you and your students could use to illustrate your Web pages or other multimedia projects.

JAZCLASS

Another source of online lesson materials comes to the Internet from Michael Furstner in Australia. His love of music and jazz shines through in his Web site project. In his words, it is an "outstanding Jazz Education site with Music Lessons on Jazz, Blues, Saxophone and music principles."

 This is another site with wonderful lesson material and sound files which you could download and use.

There are online lessons in Basic Music Theory, Jazz Theory, and Scales & Keys. There are sound files throughout the lessons as well as song files for classroom activities. Mr. Furstner also offers music courses via e-mail and music books.

JAZCLASS (c) Michael Furstner
http://www.ozemail.com.au/~jazclass/

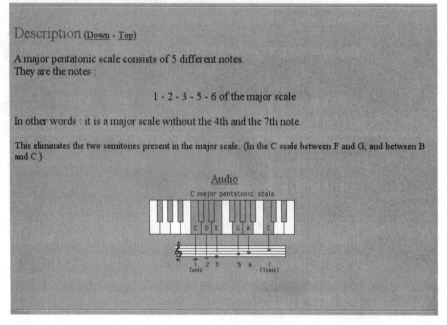

This is an example of part of one of the scales lessons.

Music Magic

Johnny Owens' index site has hundreds of music links to keep at your fingertips. It would be a terrific resource to have in your music or band classroom. It could serve as a springboard for discussions in your social studies class as well.

If you have Internet access in your classroom, you can download this single page and have resources for your students to browse as they do research about different recording artists, the history of recording studios, or different music genres.

Music Magic
http://www.geocities.com/Hollywood/Hills/5230/music2.html

You would not have ample disk space to download every Web site linked here, but this is a good example of a Web page you could download with *Web Buddy*'s Page To Go option.

You and your students will find links to sites about various artists and recording groups from Al Jolsen to Willie Nelson.

Artists Specific

Al Jolson
    Al Jolson Home Page
American Pie by Don McLean
    Lyrics and Analysis of The Song American Pie By Don McLean
Andrews Sisters
    Andrews Sisters Music
Bachelor Pad and Exotic Music Space Safari
    Bachelor Pad and Exotic Music, Artists, Discographies, RCA Stereo Action Series, Command Label,
    See Comments
Barry Manilow
    Barry Manilow Music
Benny Goodman
    Music Links
Bette Midler
    Bette Midler Music
Bill Evans
    Bill Evans Music
Bing Crosby
    Bing Crosby Music
Bobby Vee
    Visit the Bobby Vee Fan Club Page
Capitol Steps
    Parodies Comedy Music
Charlie Parker 75th Anniversary Discography
    Charlie Parker 75th Anniversary Discography
Dave Brubeck

You could assign an artist to each of your students and have them search that particular Web page for information about their artist's style of music, what albums/CD's they have released, whether they are still performing, and whether they won any awards. Then each student could create a poster about his or her artist. They could print a picture from the Web site, report about what instrument the artist plays and include other biographical information.

You could also have students research that particular artist and design an album/CD cover for one of the titles.

For teachers, this site includes a wide variety of links to sources of music. If you've been searching for that one song or album or CD, then you might want to contact some of the online music sites listed here. There are links to various recording labels and to online stores.

There are also links to sites online with sound files, such as midi files, which you could use with your re-written song lyrics Web page projects.

You could also use the Site To Go utility to download some of the classical composer sites or more current artists' sites. Have your students create multimedia presentations about them rather than just write simple reports. They could use graphics from the Web pages and audio files from other sites to illuminate their short reports. These could be done by using presentation software such as *HyperStudio* or by creating Web pages.

Other Music Web Sites:

Worldwide Internet Music Resources
http://www.music.indiana.edu/music_resources/

Children's Music List—Education
http://www.cowboy.net/~mharper/CML/Education.html

Real Player, Real Audio
http://www.real.com/

K-12 Resources for Music Educators
http://www.isd77.k12.mn.us/resources/staffpages/shirk/k12.music.html

Classical Composers Biographies
http://spight.physics.unlv.edu/bioarchives/archive.html

Classical Composer Biographies
http://www.cl.cam.ac.uk/users/mn200/music/composers.html

Music Educators National Conference Website
http://www.menc.org/

Mr. Holland's Opus—Tool Kit
http://www.amc-music.com/opus/index.htm

MidiFarm
http://www.midifarm.com/midifarm/free.asp

Midi Haven
http://www.geocities.com/Hollywood/9990/midi.html

CARNIVAL OF THE ANIMALS

Camille Saint-Saâns, born October, 9, 1835 in Paris, was a child prodigy. It is said that he composed his first piece when he was three years old. He appeared in recital at the age of seven and was playing pieces by Mozart from memory by age ten.

"Carnival of the Animals—A Grand Zoological Fantasy" for two pianos and orchestra began as a fun piece of music he composed for a party, but has become a much-loved composition. The possibilities of student activities are endless. What may have been a simple report on a composer can now be a creative project.

The composition is divided into 14 parts which focus on 12 different animals and some pianists:

1. Introduction and Royal March of the Lion
2. Hens and Roosters
3. Wild Asses
4. Tortoises
5. The Elephant
6. Kangaroos
7. The Aquarium
8. Personages with Long Ears.
9. The Cuckoo in the Depth of the Woods
10. The Aviary
11. Pianists
12. Fossils
13. The Swan
14. Finale

It is a piece of music which can be presented to students of all ages with minor adjustments in the associated activities. Quite often, with younger primary grade students, teachers have them listen to the music and draw pictures of the animals as they listen. They can also follow along to listening maps that assist in telling the story of what the music (and animals) are doing in each piece of the composition.

Are You Listening?

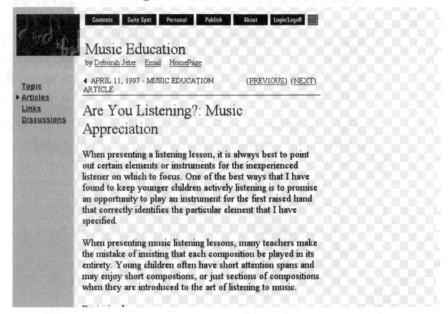

Suite 101—Music Education—April 11, 1997—Deborah Jeters
Are You Listening?
http://www.suite101.com/articles/article.cfm/1449

This article about developing listening skills includes a lesson plan, listening maps, and coloring pages for Saint-Saâns "Carnival of the Animals." In addition to maintaining her own Web page, Music, The Universal Language, Deborah is a columnist for Suite 101—Musical Education. If you would like to contact her about this activity, you are invited to e-mail her at bluesman1@earthlink.net.

You can use the Site To Go utility to download this activity and the correlating hand-outs for your students. Use it as a listening guide with a recording of "Carnival of the Animals."

You will then be able to take the files to school to print them for your students to use as you play the composition to them, one piece at a time. They can also be used as guidelines for having the students create their own listening maps.

Carnival of the Animals—CBC Radio Broadcast

Carnival of the Animals
http://www.radio.cbc.ca/programs/takefive/PERFORMANCE/L_MARSHALL/CARNIVAL.html

Ogden Nash wrote poems for each of the pieces of "Carnival of the Animals" and they have been recorded along with the composition. CBC

(Canadian Broadcast Company) As You Like It listeners were invited to write new poems to be read with the music during a contest in April of 1996. James Reid has created this Web site to share that broadcast with the public once again.

The Web site contains the poems that were winners from more than 100 which were submitted. There is also a Real Audio sound file of the complete broadcast with narration by Lois Marshall and Bramwell Tovey. The music is performed by The Festival Ensemble of the Festival of the Sound.

The Web site can be downloaded by using the Site To Go utility and setting it to take this page and follow 1 level deep. The Real Audio

links at the top of the page will connect you with the files on the server where this Web page is located. Mr. Reid has graciously created a link at the bottom of the Web page so the file with a file extension of ".ra" will download with the rest of the page and its graphics.

This file is 4.7 megabytes in size and will take a considerable amount of time to download. You should either schedule this download for a later time, or set it up to download as you are leaving your computer for a while. (At 33.6 MHz modem speed, it takes about 40 minutes to download.) Once you have downloaded that file along with the rest of the Web page, you will be able to use it while offline without having any wait time for downloading. Remember to click on the link at the bottom of the page.

You can also pause and fast-forward the music as it plays on your Real Audio player. This is important if you want to play just one part of the music, or if you want to skip over the poem and have them listen to each piece without hearing the poem first.

Another option would be to have the students listen to each piece without telling them which animal it represents. List all the animals randomly and let them take turns guessing which animal Saint-Saâns is representing.

Once they have listened to a piece, have them each write a poem to accompany it. After they have all written their own poems, you might have someone judge them. Then make your own recordings of the poems and music.

With a class of 28–30 students, you might want to pick a poem from each student so that each piece of the music has two representative poems on the recording. Each student can also narrate his or her own poem in the recording. Copies of these could be sent home to the parents so they can hear what you are doing in your class.

Program Music by Camille Saint Saâns

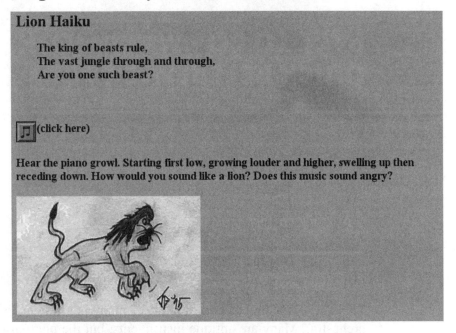

Program Music by Camille Saint-Saâns
http://busboy.sped.ukans.edu/~music/carnival/

This Web site is a compilation of student work. There is a history of Saint-Saâns with hypertext links to major points of interest in the report along with children's artwork and haiku for the various pieces. Each of those pages has a button to click and hear a sound file of that part of the composition.

This would be an easy project template to follow if you wanted to scan in students' artwork. Have them include it with poems written by another class in a school Web page or multimedia project.

You could also download some of the other resources listed and provide the students with graphics and photographs of animals and musical instruments. The students could print the images of the correct animals for each piece and also find representatives of the musical instrument that represents the animal.

University of Michigan—Instrument Encyclopedia

Welcome to the Instrument Encyclopedia!

Beginning with more than 140 artifacts from the Stearns Collection at the University of Michigan, this resource features musical instruments from around the world. Explore the diversity and creativity of musical traditions as you browse our gallery or search for a favorite instrument

Please choose one of the following search options:

 Alphabetical

Instruments organized alphabetically under each of four groupings: Electronic, Percussion, String, Winds

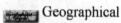 Geographical

By country of origin. Start your search by selecting a continent of interest on a clickable world map (Note: not all instruments in the Encyclopedia will be found here)

Welcome to the Instrument Encyclopedia!
http://www.si.umich.edu/CHICO/MHN/enclpdia.html

This encyclopedia has photographs of many instruments of the orchestra. Many are antique instruments, but the photographs could be used by the students to show which instrument is being heard.

Clarinet in B flat

Origins:	London, England; Key, maker	
Date:	ca 1835	
Materials:	Dark wood (rosewood?), sterling silver, metal, ivory mountings	

Collection Stearns, no 917

Description

This clarinet, crafted in London ca the 1830s, is made from rosewood or a similar wood and has 13 metal keys. The rosewood mouthpiece is not original; a number of instruments from the Stearns collection are composites, with newer elements (mouthpieces, for example) replacing worn or missing parts. Length, 60.3 cm

More information on Clarinet

Each instrument is identified and described on its own Web page. If you click on the thumbnail photograph, there is a larger photograph as well.

Sounds of the World's Animals

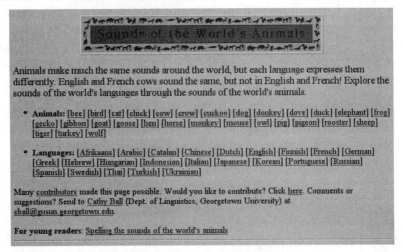

Sounds of the World's Animals
http://www.georgetown.edu/cball/animals/animals.html

Cathy Ball, with the Dept. of Linguistics at Georgetown University, created this Web site to illustrate the different ways the names of animal sounds are pronounced in different countries around the world.

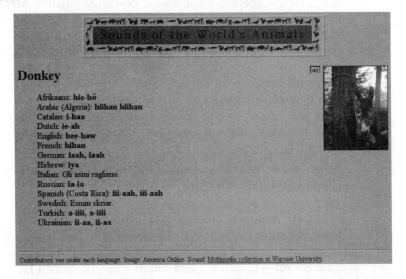

For each animal, she has included a picture, the pronunciations, and sometimes a sound file of the animal actually making its noise.

Download selected images using the Page To Go utility. These could be incorporated into the student activities if they were making Web pages or multimedia presentations. With all of these resources, a student could have a Web page for a piece of the music with a graphic of the animal (either hand drawn or downloaded), a poem for the piece, and a sound file for the music and for the animal.

Other Carnival of the Animals Web Sites:

Carnival of the Animals Merchandise
(several audio files you can download)
http://www.iagmusic.com/carnival.htm

Carnival of the Animals
(Real Audio excerpts which will download and play on your computer—use Site To Go and take this page and go one level deep—must have RealAudio player on computer)
http://nic.uakom.sk/audiobox/1075.html

Other Camille Saint-Saâns Web Sites:

Classical Net
http://www.classical.net/music/composer/index.html

Camille Saint Saâns
http://www.classical.net/music/comp.lst/st-saens.html

Classical Net
http://www.futurenet.com/classicalnet/

Camille Saint Saâns Biography
(sound sample files)
http://www.futurenet.com/classicalnet/reference/composers/saint-saens.html

French Composers—Ravel and Saint Saâns
http://Weber.u.washington.edu/~sbode/music/french2.html

CultureNet—Camille Saint Saâns
http://www.culturefinder.com/burkat/camille_saint-saens_links.htm

Danse Macabre Web Sites:

A Lesson Plan for Halloween
(lesson and sound files in .mov format)
http://pages.nyu.edu/~btt200/lesson.html

Dr. Steve Hajioff's Midi Collection
(contains Danse Macabre midi file)
http://www.ftech.net/~sawbones/midi.htm

Other Composer Web Sites:

Ed's Composer Links
http://members.aol.com/Orquesta/home.html

Classically tongue-tied
USA Today article about pronouncing difficult classical composers'
names
http://usatoday.com/life/enter/music/lem268.htm

Other Instruments of the Orchestra Web Sites:

Symphony Nova Scotia
http://reseau.chebucto.ns.ca/Culture/SNS/index.html

Edinburgh University Collection of Historic Musical Instruments
http://www.music.ed.ac.uk/euchmi/

Electronic Picture Gallery
(photographs of historic instruments—with enlarged graphics
available)
http://www.music.ed.ac.uk/euchmi/cat/vol3.html

Indianapolis Symphony Orchestra
http://www.in.net/iso/

Creating the Educated Listener
(composer time line—puzzle pages for identifying musical
instruments)
http://www.in.net/iso/ISOEDpg.html

Musical Instruments—illustrations and descriptions
http://reseau.chebucto.ns.ca/Culture/SNS/instrum1.html

Other Sound File Web Sites:

Midi Haven
(organized by genre and artist—choose Classical A-H for Danse
Macabre—several versions of "Dance")
http://www.geocities.com/Hollywood/9990/midi.html

Jack's Shack—Midi Files
http://jacks-shack.xtn.net/music.html

Midi File
http://midibiz.w1.com/mcat/zsaintsa.htm

Other Animal Graphics Web Sites:

Icon Bazaar—Animal Images
(download with the Page To Go utility—there are many icon images
on the page)
http://www.iconbazaar.com/animals/

DH Art Gallery—animated for Web page use
http://www.dgsys.com/~hollyb/aniother.html

Gallery Animals—photos
http://www.meyercs.com/galanimals.html

APPENDIX A

Quick Reference Cards

The following set of cards have been provided so that you can reproduce them and post them near your computer to use as clues for the three utilities that you will use most often:

- Page To Go
- Site To Go
- Convert (Windows 95) or Translate (Macintosh) File

APPENDIX B

Copyright Issues

This appendix covers several issues relating to copyrights and information on the Internet.

- Web site management
- Contacting Webmasters for permission to download
- Citing electronic resources

QUICK REFERENCE CARDS
PAGE TO GO—MACINTOSH

1. Open your Web browser software (ex: *Netscape* or *Internet Explorer*)

2. Locate the Web page you want to download.

3. Start *Web Buddy* Tool Bar.

4. Click on the Page To Go button on the toolbar.

5. Select a category or create a new category where you want this Web page to be downloaded.

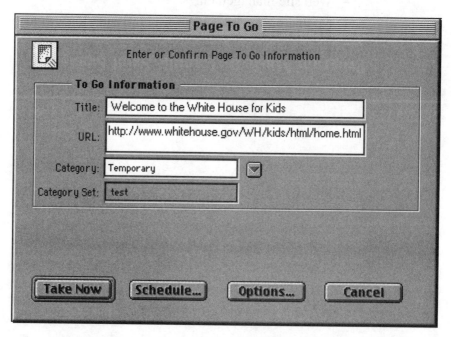

6. Click on Take Now to download the Web page.

QUICK REFERENCE CARDS
SITE TO GO—MACINTOSH

1. Open your Web browser software (ex: *Netscape* or *Internet Explorer*).

2. Locate the Web page you want to download.

3. Start *Web Buddy* Tool Bar.

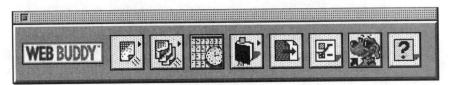

4. Click on the Site To Go button on the toolbar.

5. Select a category or create a new category where you want this Web site to be downloaded.

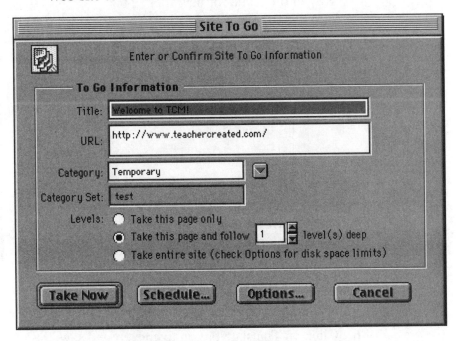

6. Click on Take Now to download the Web site.

QUICK REFERENCE CARDS
TRANSLATE FILE—MACINTOSH

1. Open your Web browser software (ex: *Netscape* or *Internet Explorer*)
2. Locate the Web page you want to download.
3. Start *Web Buddy* Tool Bar.

4. Click on the translate button on the toolbar.
5. Choose folder where you want new file saved.

   Select word processor format.

   Key in file name for new file.

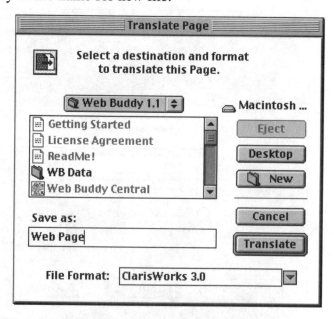

6. Click on Translate button to convert and save the Web page.

QUICK REFERENCE CARDS
PAGE TO GO—WINDOWS

1. Open your Web browser software (ex: *Netscape* or *Internet Explorer*).

2. Locate the Web page you want to download.

3. Start *Web Buddy* Tool Bar.

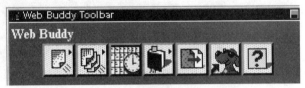

4. Click on the Page To Go button on the toolbar.

5. Select a category or create a new category where you want this Web page to be downloaded.

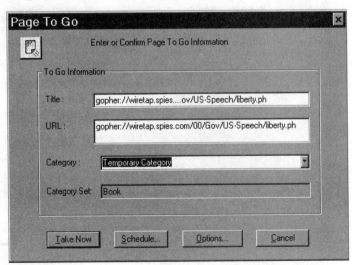

6. Click on Take Now to download the Web page.

QUICK REFERENCE CARDS
SITE TO GO—WINDOWS

1. Open your Web browser software (ex: *Netscape* or *Internet Explorer*).

2. Locate the Web page you want to download.

3. Start *Web Buddy* Tool Bar.

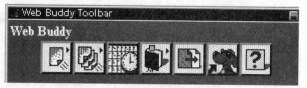

4. Click on the Site To Go button on the toolbar.

5. Select a category or create a new category where you want this Web site to be downloaded.

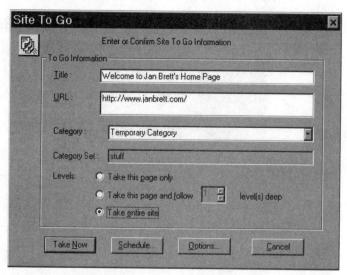

6. Click on Take Now to download the Web site.

QUICK REFERENCE CARDS
CONVERT FILE—WINDOWS

1. Open your Web browser software (ex: *Netscape* or *Internet Explorer*).
2. Locate the Web page you want to download.
3. Start *Web Buddy* Tool Bar.

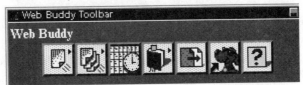

4. Click on the Convert button on the toolbar.

5. Choose directory/folder where you want new file saved.

   Select word processor format.

   Key in file name for new file.

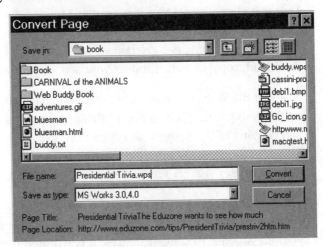

6. Click on Convert button to convert and save Web page.

COPYRIGHT ISSUES

This is probably one of the most talked-about and least-understood topics in conversations about using the Internet and Web sites. As teachers, we have assumed that a "fair use" ruling applied to us. We know that resource materials we purchased for classroom use could be duplicated for student use, but the "rules" about other things like newspaper articles or cartoon images are unclear.

The assumption that we can copy these materials for classroom use falls under that "fair use" rule. This has applied to print materials such as news articles, editorial cartoons, or a few pages from a book—things which the teacher felt he or she needed to illustrate a "teachable moment." The copies the teacher makes should not cause the author to lose potential income. The time it would take to write and ask the author for permission to make the copies would be too long for the content to be used in the lesson.

Now—enter the Internet. Because this material is online, does it mean that it is "fair game?" Is everything on the net free to copy and use? Because it is published in electronic form, is it automatically in the "public domain?"

Probably not.

Unless it clearly states that it is available to be copied or that the graphics and text are public domain material, it is best to assume that the material belongs to someone, is copyrighted, and is not "up for grabs" for you to download, copy, or transmit over your school's intranet.

Many of the Web sites featured in this book have copyright policies posted on the Web pages. Quite a few of them give permission for downloading and copying of their pages for educational use. Some of them ask that you ask them for permission before copying or downloading any part of their pages—for any use. A few of them don't say anything.

The best advice we can give you is to ask everyone. It is simply common courtesy to ask permission before you download these Web pages to use in your classroom. In some instances, it is required that you ask.

KEEPING IT LEGAL:

Questions Arising out of Web Site Management

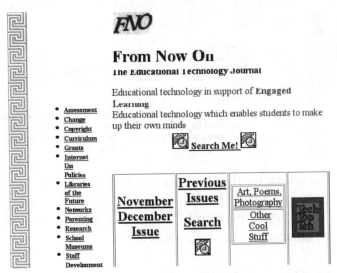

From Now On—The Educational Technology Journal
http://fromnowon.org/

Dr. Jamie McKenzie, publisher of From Now On, has written a
terrific article about several copyright issues. He includes examples
of issues you might encounter during your use of the Internet in your
classroom in the form of case studies.

The case studies deal with use of photographs downloaded from a
Web site, use of CD clipart, and content of student-created Web sites.
In the cases of the graphics, again, the best policy is to write to Web
site owners and ask permission to use their materials in your
educational project.

From Now On gives permission to download materials from their
Web site for educational use. This means that you may download or
print copies of this article to read at a later date or to share with your
principal and fellow teachers. This does not mean that you can
download this material and post it on your school's network or Web
site.

The Copyright Website
http://www.benedict.com/homepage.htm

1976 US copyright act
http://www.law.cornell.edu/usc/17/overview.html

Information Infrastructure Task Force Working Group on Intellectual
Property Rights White Paper
http://www.uspto.gov

Transcopyright
By Ted Nelson
http://www.world3.com/meme1/nelson2.html

Copyright Policy: Materials published in From Now On may be
duplicated for educational, non-profit school district use only. All other
uses, transmissions and duplications are prohibited unless permission is
granted expressly

The policy for the Web pages at From Now On are clearly stated in a
Copyright Policy posted at the bottom of the pages. Many pages
simply have a hypertext link which leads you to a Web page
explaining the copyright policy.

The Copyright Website:

This Web site, created by Benedict O'Mahoney, also gives you
current information about copyright issues. They deal with print
issues as well as those surrounding Web site use.

The Copyright Website
http://www.benedict.com/

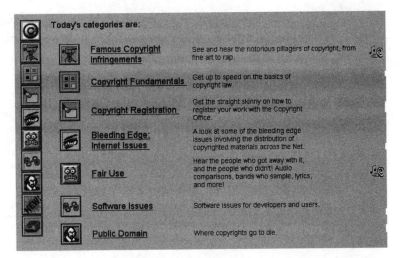

Before your students download and use any of the graphics in their projects, you can use some of the famous infringement cases as teaching materials as you teach your class about copyright rules. These are mostly current copying issues of music and art—instances where someone made money from someone else's work without having approval to use it.

How Do You Find The Webmaster?

So—now that you know you should, how do you go about finding the author, publisher, or Webmaster of a Web page? You can usually find the e-mail address of the Webmaster, publisher, or writer of a Web page in a prominent place on the page. It can posted at the bottom of a welcome page, or with the copyright policy.

In the case of From Now On, the information is posted on the opening page of the Web site.

From Now On is published by Jamie McKenzie

mckenzie@fromnowon.org
Network 609
901 Twelfth Street
Bellingham, WA 98225
360-647-8759

Mr. O'Mahoney has made it easy to contact him as well. He has also made the copyright status available to his readers by posting this message at the bottom of his opening Web page.

Comments

Thanks for visiting The Copyright Website. This site is continuously updated and expanded, so check back soon for the latest changes.

If you have any comments, notice any glaring inaccuracies, or would like to forward any relevant information concerning The Copyright Website WWW service, please send e-mail to: *comments@benedict.com*

Copyright © 1995-1997 Benedict O'Mahoney

Look for messages like these on Web sites you want to download for use in your classroom.

Each of the featured Web sites in this book gave permission for screen images to be included as part of instructions to you, the reader, for finding the Web site and seeing what is included. They have not given carte blanche permission for you to download their pages. They would probably like to hear from you and find out what you will be doing with their site in your classes.

How Do You Ask Permission?

This is the easy part. Remember asking mom or dad for permission to borrow the car or that favorite sweater or a book? This is the same thing, but easier. You're already online and looking at their Web page. You've already found the copyright information and the name and e-mail address of a contact person. So, just drop them a short e-mail, tell them who you are, let them know you're a teacher, and explain how and why you want to use their Web site.

If you don't have your own personal e-mail account, sign up for one with a free e-mail service such as:
Hotmail (at **http://www.hotmail.com**). Once your e-mail account is active, you're ready to start asking permission.

Sample E-mail for Asking Permission

Dear Webmaster,

I am a teacher at _____ School and my class will be studying _____. I found your Web site while browsing the Internet and would like to use it (or specify which part) with my students.

I would like permission to use an offline browser, *Web Buddy*, to download your Web pages to a disk so that I can use them on my computer in my classroom which is not online. I will make sure that credit for ownership of the Web pages remains with you.

Thank you for your assistance and for the information in your Web site.

Sincerely,

Teacher

Citing Electronic Sources

Now that you and your students have gotten permission to use information from the Internet—Web pages, gopher site contents, e-mail communications— how do you cite the reference in your work?

There are several sources online which show examples of bibliography entries for various types of electronic works. There are minor differences among them, but you should agree on one standard version in your school. Teach all your students the same version.

The APA (American Psychological Association) and MLA (Modern Language Association) guidelines are posted on several Web sites. The underlying guideline is that you will need the URL and a copyright or "last updated" date (or date downloaded) from each Web page you wish to cite.

Electronic Sources: APA Style of Citation

PLEASE NOTE: Follow recommended patterns given in the *Publication Manual of the American Psychological Association*, 4th edition, for indentation of items in a "Reference List."

Individual Works

Basic forms, commercial supplier, and using an Internet protocol.

Author/editor. (Year). *Title* (edition), [Type of medium]. Producer (optional). Available Supplier/Database identifier or number [Access date].

Author/editor. (Year). *Title* (edition), [Type of medium]. Producer (optional). Available Protocol (if applicable): Site/Path/File [Access date]

Examples.

- *Oxford English dictionary computer file: On compact disc* (2nd ed.), [CD-ROM]. (1992). Available: Oxford UP [1995, May 27]

- Pritzker, T. J. (No date). *An Early fragment from central Nepal* [Online]. Available: http://www.ingress.com/~astanart/pritzker/pritzker.html [1995, June 8]

APA Style of Citation
http://www.uvm.edu/~ncrane/estyles/apa.html

MLA Style of Citation
http://www.uvm.edu/~ncrane/estyles/mla.html

In both of these APA and MLA pages, Nancy Crane has given basic guidelines and examples of how that would look with a real information source.

Guide for Citing Electronic Information

Kurt Wagner at the Sarah Byrd Askew Library at William Paterson University in Wayne, NJ created a simple table which sorts out the various common electronic resources you will be citing. Examples are given for books, journals, and magazines from these electronic media:

> Online/CD Network
> E-mail
> FTP
> Gopher
> Telnet
> WWW

Guide for Citing Electronic Information
Based on Electronic Style: A Guide for Citing Electronic Information,
by Li, X. & Crane, N. (1993). Westport: Meckler

Some general rules:

- The date provided in electronic information is not necessarily the original date of publication for the resource. The date may be when it was added to the database.
- The goal of the citation is to allow the information to be retrieved again. Keep this in mind. Check to make sure that the information you provide will allow a repeat of your work
- Punctuation and capitalization, especially in the "electronic address" of the resource, should appear just as it is used in the database

Guide for Citing Electronic Information

Sarah Byrd Askew Library
http://www.wilpaterson.edu/wpcpages/library/citing.htm

	Telnet	Truck, F. (1992, June). [Abstract of Archaeopteryx]. *ArtCom* [Online]. Available Telnet: gopher.tc.umn.edu Directory: Libraries/Newspapers, Magazines, and Newsletters/Art/ArtCom File V.1 N.3 June 92
	WWW	Leob, P.R. (1994, September-October). Greeks and granolas and steeps and slackers. *Mother Jones Magazine* [Online]. Available HTTP: http://www.mojones.com/SO94/toc.html File: GREEKS AND GRANOLAS AND STEEPS AND SLACKERS
Electronic Mail	Personal	Corliss, B. (1992, September 16). *News from Seattle* [e-mail to X. Li], [Online]. Available e-mail: XLI@UVMVM.UVM.EDU

This is a good guideline for presenting your school's accepted form for citing resources. As you download materials from the Internet, you need to remember to record the URL and the date of the material. Keep this in a data file or in a notebook near your computer so that students can access it as they use the materials you have downloaded.

Other Citing Resources Web Sites:

Guide for Citing Electronic Resources
http://www.wilpaterson.edu/wpcpages/library/citing.htm

Other Copyright Issue Web Sites:

U.S. Copyright Office—Library of Congress
http://lcWeb.loc.gov/copyright/

Copyright Tips and Issues
http://www.siec.k12.in.us/~west/online/copy.htm

Copyright for Educators
http://lcWeb.loc.gov/copyright/circs/circ21

ILTguide to Copyright
http://www.ilt.columbia.edu/projects/copyright/index.html

School Board Policy on Internet Use
Bellingham, WA
http://www.bham.wednet.edu/policies.htm

GLOSSARY

Bookmark—A way to store a Web address (URL) without having to write it down to remember it. Your browser can store bookmarks. *Web Buddy* can also keep track of bookmarks for you in categories you specify.

Browser—The program that allows you to access and read hypertext documents on a network or on the World Wide Web. *Netscape Navigator* is one type of browser.

Category Set—A set or grouping of categories that is created and maintained within the To Go Manager in *Web Buddy* Central. It is a way to help you organize your downloaded Web pages.

Convert (Windows Version)—This utility allows you to turn a Web page and/or graphics into formats that you can use with your word processing program.

E-mail (Electronic Mail)—A system for sending text messages from one person to another via computer.

HTML (HyperText Markup Language)—The coding language used to create hypertext documents for use on the World Wide Web.

HTTP (HyperText Transfer Protocol)—The protocol for moving hypertext files across the Internet.

Hypertext—Any text that contains links to other documents—words or phrases in the document are usually highlighted or underlined and can be chosen by a reader to have another screen or document appear.

Internet—The collection of over 60,000 inter-connected networks.

Intranet—A private network inside a company or organization.

ISP (Internet Service Provider)—A company or organization that provides access to the Internet in some form, usually for money.

GLOSSARY *(cont.)*

Manager—In *Web Buddy* Central, a manager is the main storage area for its accompanying toolbar utility. For instance, the To Go Manager is where you find all the pages and sites you've downloaded using the To Go utilities.

Midi—A music file format.

Temporary Category—This category is used as a holding place when you download Web pages and Web sites unless you designate a specific category you have created.

Translate (Macintosh Version)—See **Convert**.

To Go—In *Web Buddy*, taking a page or site "to go" is downloading it to your computer so you can browse through it later.

URL (Uniform Resource Locator)—This is the standard address of any site on the Internet that is part of the World Wide Web.

***Web Buddy* Toolbar**—The floating toolbar that launches with your Web browser to give you easy access to *Web Buddy*'s utilities.

***Web Buddy* Central**—The main application area of *Web Buddy* where all your pages, bookmarks, schedules, etc. are stored.

WWW (World Wide Web)—The vast network of hypertext servers (HTTP servers) which are the servers that allow text, graphics, sound files, etc. to be mixed together.

INDEX

INDEX *(cont.)*

INDEX *(cont.)*

INDEX *(cont.)*

Web Buddy Technical Support

For Web Buddy technical support contact any one of the following:

DataViz Web site: **http://www.dataviz.com**
Phone: 203-268-0030
Fax: 203-268-4345
